D0246930
JVC
£5.50

WORLD CUP '98

JUNE 15th 1998

ENGLAND 2-0 TUNISIA (HT: 1-0)

ENGLAND: Seaman, Campbell, Le Saux, Adams, Southgate, Ince, Batty, Scholes, Anderton, Shearer, Sheringham (sub: Owen)
Scorers: Shearer (43mins), Scholes (89mins)
TUNISIA: El Ouaer, Clayton, Badra, S Trabelsi, Boukadida, H Trabelsi (sub: Thanet), Godhbane, Chihi, Souayah (sub: Baya), Sellimi, Ben Slimane (sub: Ben Younes)
REFEREE: M Okada (Japan)
ATT: 54,587 (Marseille)

Man United's Paul Scholes made the entire nation forget about the missing Paul Gascoigne as he turned on a fantastic five star display to inspire a comfortable England victory against the mediocre Tunisians. Scholes linked midfield and attack superbly, was involved in just about every important England move and capped his performance off perfectly with a wonder strike.

England's first goal of the tournament, however, was scored by Newcastle super striker Alan Shearer just before half-time, heading past 'keeper El Ouaer from a well placed Graeme Le Saux free-kick. It was Shearer's 14th international goal in just 17 games. Teddy Sheringham was also unlucky not to get on the scoresheet following his brilliantly taken long range dipping volley which El Ouaer did well to block.

If anything England's second half dominance was even greater with Paul Ince and David Batty effortlessly controlling the midfield while Gareth Southgate and Sol Campbell snuffed out any chance of a Tunisian recovery at the back. But it was that man Scholes who continued to impress more than any other member of Hoddle's side – playing inch perfect passes, tackling back and going on mazy Gazza-like runs whenever the mood took him. The 23-year-old had clearly taken to international football like a duck to water and seemed ready to make a big impact in the tournament as a whole. Scholes polished off a glittering display a few minutes from the end with a terrific goal. Finding himself on the edge of the opposition's penalty box with little space to move, Scholes twisted and turned the Tunisian defence before curling his shot beyond 'keeper El Ouaer into the net. It was one of the best goals of the tournament up to that point and a sign that England weren't going to have to rely on Shearer to get them goals.

ROUND ONE ENGLAND v TUNISIA

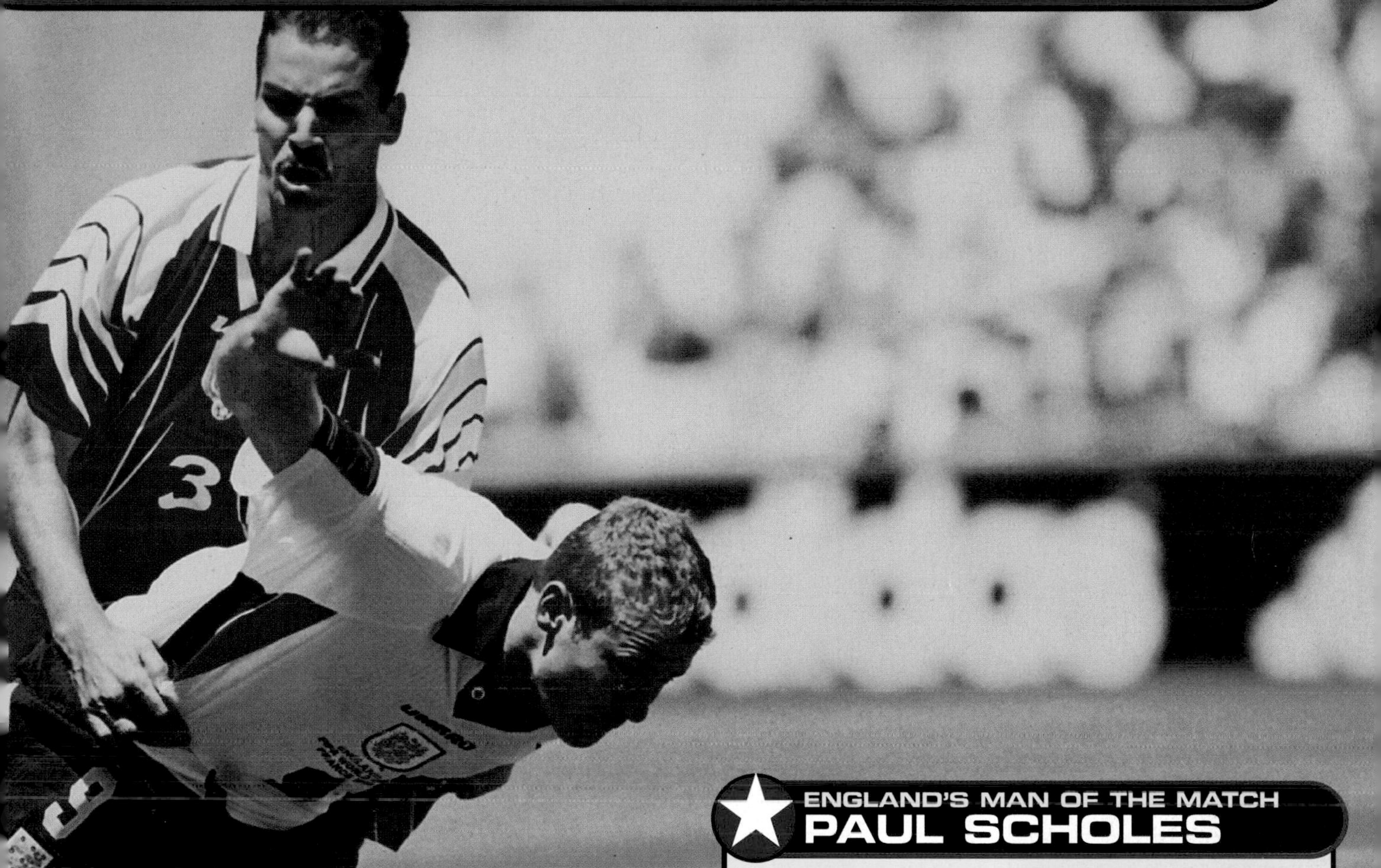

ENGLAND'S MAN OF THE MATCH
PAUL SCHOLES

Playing just behind Shearer and Sheringham, Scholes was England's most potent attacking threat right from the first whistle. The Tunisian defence found his late runs into the box impossible to handle and his skill on the ball equally problematic. His goal capped a wonderful display for the 23-year-old Man United star.

WORLD CUP '98

ROUND ONE SCOTLAND v NORWAY

XXTH JUNE 1998:
SCOTLAND (0) 1 - 1 (0) NORWAY

SCOTLAND: Leighton, Boyd, Calderwood (sub: Weir), Hendry, Burley, Collins, Dailly, Lambert, Durie, Gallacher, Jackson (sub: McNamara)
Scorer: Burley (66mins)
NORWAY: Grodas, Berg (sub: Halle), Bjornebye, Eggen, Johnsen, Strand, Rekdal, Solbakken, H. Flo (sub: Jakobsen), T. Flo, Riseth (sub: Ostenstad)
Scorer: H. Flo (46mins)
REFEREE: L Vagner (Hungary)
ATT: 30,236 (Bordeaux)

It was more bad luck for the Scots in a match they dominated for long periods without making that superiority count. Craig Brown's men easily had the best of a lifeless Norwegian side in the first half but must have cursed their poor finishing in the dressing room at half-time. Derby's Christian Dailly had his side's best chance to open the scoring when he met John Collins' free-kick with a header that went wide. Gordon Durie also failed in front of goal as his effort hit the side netting. Durie also had a clear penalty turned down by the referee after Stig Bjornebye upended him in the box.

Despite being goalless at the break, the tartan army must have felt the game was Scotland's for the taking but once again Craig Brown's men proved to be their own worst enemies. Barely a minute after the restart Norway went one up. Riseth charged down the left and was given far too much space for his cross by defender Calderwood. The unmarked Harvard Flo met the ball with his head and suddenly Scotland's World Cup dream hung in tatters.

As they had against Brazil, however, the Scots mounted a stunning fightback, laying siege to the Norway goal as they searched for an equaliser and a France '98 lifeline. The breakthrough came in the 66th minute when substitute David Weir found the advancing Craig Burley with a superb throughball. Burley, with time to steady himself and pick his spot, lobbed 'keeper Grodas expertly. After that the Scots went hell for leather after a winner. Burley produced a superb save from Grodas following some good work from Durie, but the Norwegian defence refused to buckle and at the final whistle the Scots were once again wondering what might have been. Only a good result against Morocco and a Brazilian win over Norway would now be enough to keep them in the competition.

SCOTLAND'S MAN OF THE MATCH
CRAIG BURLEY

It was his goal which handed Scotland a World Cup lifeline in the second half and he almost grabbed a winner for Craig Brown's men towards the end. The Scottish manager had switched Burley from his position at full-back in the Brazil game to a more favoured berth in midfield against Norway – clearly, it did the trick, as he was superb throughout.

WORLD CUP '98

JUNE 22nd 1998

ENGLAND 1-2 ROMANIA (HT: 0-0)

ENGLAND: Seaman, Adams, Campbell, Le Saux, Neville, Anderton, Batty, Ince (sub: Beckham), Scholes, Shearer, Sheringham (sub: Owen)
Scorer: Owen (83mins)
ROMANIA: Stelea, Ciobotariu, Petrescu, Gica Popescu, Filipescu, Galca, Hagi (sub: Stanga sub: Marinescu), Munteanu, Gabriel Popescu, Ilie, Moldovan (sub: Lacatus)
Scorer: Moldovan (47), Petrescu (90)
REFEREE: M Batta (France)
ATT: 37,000 (Montpellier)

England may have considered themselves one of the best international sides in the world coming into this match but they were given a footballing lesson by group seeds Romania – and most particularly by two players from the English Premiership itself!

The first half might have ended 0-0 but, in truth, Romania could and probably should have been at least a goal to the good by then, such was the England side's lack of quality. Boss Glenn Hoddle had once again chosen to leave out Liverpool's Michael Owen and United's David Beckham in favour of Teddy Sheringham and David Batty. As a result England seemed to lack ideas up front and a spark of creativity in midfield, despite Paul Scholes' presence. Romanian youngster Adrian Ilie had the best chance of the half when his expertly executed chip grazed the England bar, while Paul Ince was carried off with an ankle injury, paving the way for Beckham's World Cup debut after just over half an hour.

As the second period began it was clear the English defence hadn't learned its lesson and was punished for it when Romanian veteran Gheorghe Hagi wrong footed Adams with a brilliant pass, leaving Coventry City striker Viorel Moldovan with a simple finish.

Twenty-five minutes later Glenn Hoddle finally introduced Michael Owen into the proceedings and it wasn't long before he'd restored some English pride with a superbly taken equaliser. Beckham and Shearer linked up well down the right, the latter firing in an inch perfect cross for Owen to thump past Stelea. Sadly, the English revival was short lived and, as the final whistle beckoned, Chelsea star Dan Petrescu hustled club team-mate Graeme Le Saux off the ball and placed a shot through David Seaman's legs for 2-1. Michael Owen hit the post seconds later but it wasn't enough to save Hoddle's men from defeat.

ENGLAND'S MAN OF THE MATCH
MICHAEL OWEN

At just 18 years of age Michael Owen made a commanding start to his World Cup career. His eye for goal and confidence on the ball clearly frightened the Romanians, who'd seemed so cool, composed and impregnable before he made his 73rd minute entrance. Owen's goal was superb and he'd have become a national hero had his last gasp strike gone in.

ROUND ONE ENGLAND v ROMANIA

WORLD CUP '98

SCOTLAND'S MAN OF THE MATCH
PAUL LAMBERT

The Celtic man had an exemplary tournament even if his country didn't. His hard working performances at the heart of the Scottish midfield won him many admirers and even when the chips were down against the Moroccans he battled on, breaking up attack after attack and creating chances for the Scottish forwards.

ROUND ONE SCOTLAND v MOROCCO

JUNE 23rd 1998

SCOTLAND 0-3 MOROCCO (HT:0-1)

SCOTLAND: Leighton, McNamara (sub: T. McKinlay), Boyd, Hendry, Weir, Burley, Collins, Lambert, Dailly, Gallacher, Durie (sub: Booth)
MOROCCO: Benzekri, Saber (sub: Rossi), Naybet, Abrami, Triki, Hadji, Amzine (sub: Azzouzi), Chippo (sub: Sellami), El Khalej, Hadda, Bassir
Scorers: Bassir (22mins, 85mins), Hadda (47mins)
REFEREE: A M Bujssaim (United Arab Emirates)
ATT: 35,500 (Saint-Etienne)

It was a night of heartbreak for the Scots who needed to win to keep their World Cup hopes alive. Sadly, it wasn't to be and the Moroccans, who earlier in the tournament had shown their class in a 2-2 draw with Norway, swept to victory mostly thanks to two superb goals from Salaheddine Bassir.

The classy Moroccans opened the scoring on 22 minutes when that man Bassir pounced on a rare defensive error by Colin Hendry and beat Jim Leighton with a fierce shot at his near post. Scotland could find little in their armoury to hit back although John Collins and Paul Lambert once again produced top-notch performances in midfield, combining well early on to set up Gordon Durie who's weak effort was easily smothered by 'keeper Benzekri. Durie had another couple of chances to level the score in the first half but both were ruined by his poor finishing.

Scotland's World Cup aspirations were all but dead and buried within two minutes of the restart, when Abdeljilil Hadda notched Morocco's second, a clever lob which totally foxed the otherwise excellent Jim Leighton. The Scottish 'keeper managed to parry Hadda's effort but could only stumble back in horror as the ball deflected off his hands and looped into the net.

Scotland's evening descended into further misery just after the second goal when Craig Burley was red carded for a clumsy tackle on Bassir. It was all one way traffic from then on with the Moroccans adding a third goal five minutes from time when Bassir's effort cannoned off Colin Hendry past Leighton. At the final whistle the Scottish players sank to their knees in utter misery while Morocco were equally gutted. The African side thought they'd qualified ahead of Norway for the Second Round but a late winner for the Scandinavians against Brazil meant that they had gone through instead.

WORLD CUP '98

26TH JUNE 1998

ENGLAND 2-0 COLOMBIA (HT: 2-0)

ENGLAND: Seaman, Neville, Adams, Campbell, Anderton (sub: Lee), Le Saux, Ince (sub: Batty), Scholes (sub: McManaman), Beckham, Owen, Shearer.
Scorers: Anderton (22mins), Beckham (30mins)
COLOMBIA: Mondragon, Carbrera, Bermudez, Palacios, Moreno, Serna (sub: Aristizabal), Lozano, Rincon, Valderrama, Preciado (sub: Valencia), De Avila (sub: Ricard)
REFEREE: Brizio Carter (Mexico)
ATT: 41,000 (Lens)

England resurrected their World Cup hopes with a fine performance against a Colombian side who had plenty of skillful individuals but rarely combined well as a team. Even the legendary Valderrama had a poor game as his team-mates crumbled before England's attacking prowess and defensive impregnability. England dominated proceedings from the off with Darren Anderton the main orchestrator of Colombian misery. His runs down the right wing were a constant thorn in the South American team's side and it was he who opened the scoring after just 22 minutes, spinning in the penalty area to smash home a fine volley past 'keeper Mondragon.

Before the game the big talking point of England's World Cup had been manager Hoddle's decision to leave Michael Owen and David Beckham on the bench. Many fans and pundits had felt England would have at least avoided defeat against the Romanians had the dynamic duo been on the pitch for the entire 90 minutes. Bowing to this public pressure, Hoddle wisely decided to start with the impressive youngsters as England went looking for goals to ensure their safe passage to the Second Round. The manager's rethink paid off after half an hour when England won a free-kick 25 yards from goal, the result of an ill-timed challenge on the fit-again Paul Ince. Up stepped Beckham and his brilliant curling strike sailed over the Colombian wall, past Mondragon, into the net. The goal all but confirmed England's victory, their first over a South American side in a competitive game since the defeat of Paraguay during the World Cup in Mexico in 1986.

Colombia made changes in the second half as they went looking for goals. But it was all too little too late as England comfortably held on to book their place against Argentina in the knockout stage of the tournament.

ENGLAND'S MAN OF THE MATCH
DAVID BECKHAM

Becks had had to wait two games to make his first World Cup start but more than made up for lost time with a thrilling midfield display capped by that wonderful free-kick goal. Along with Anderton and Owen, Beckham seemed to terrify the Colombian defence every time he had the ball and his passing was excellent.

ROUND ONE ENGLAND v COLOMBIA

FRANCE 98
COUPE DU MONDE

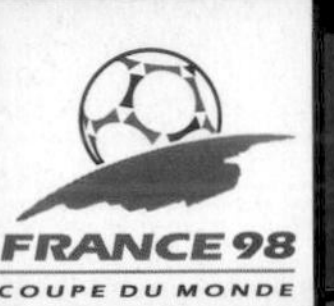

WORLD CUP '98

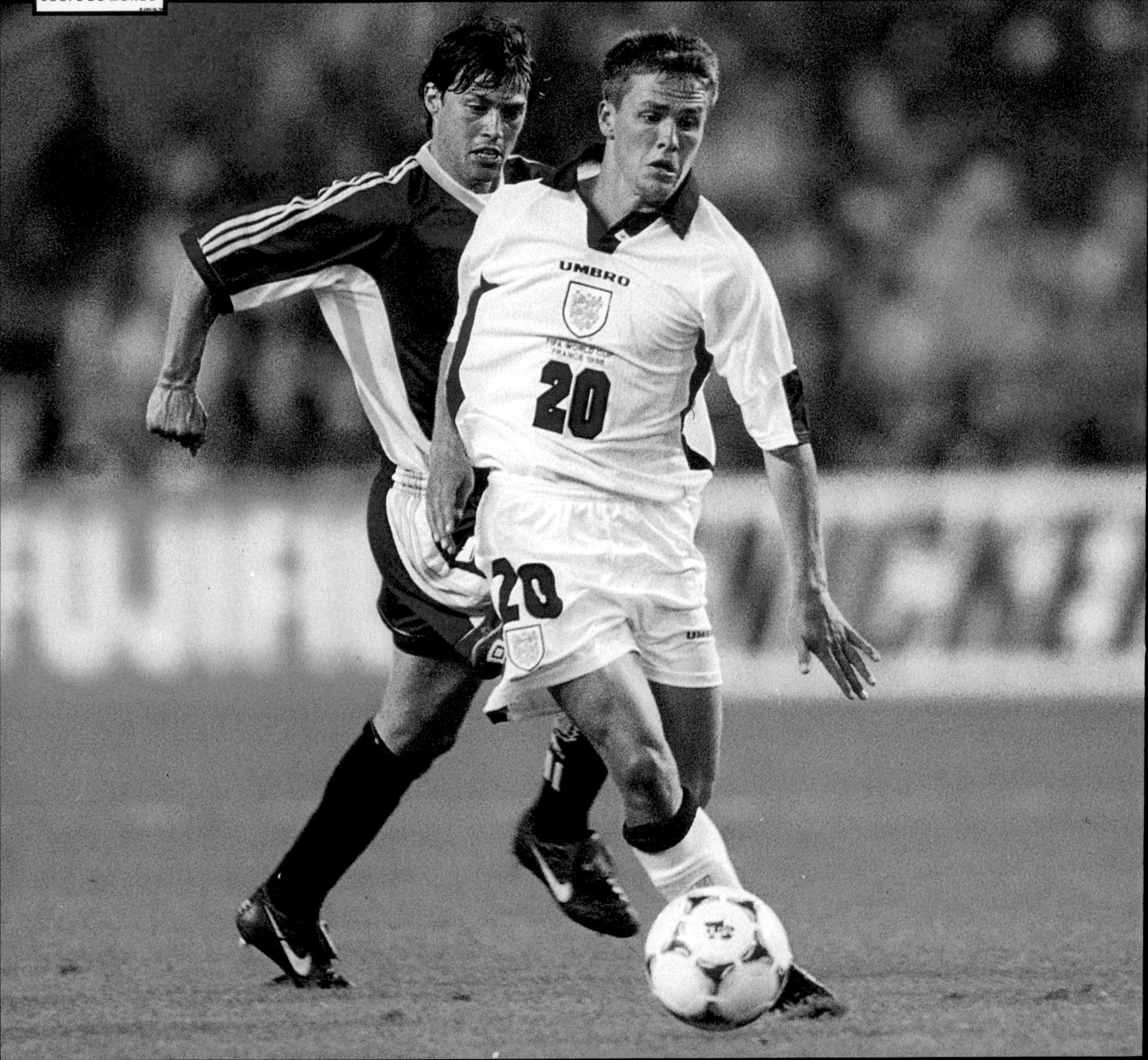

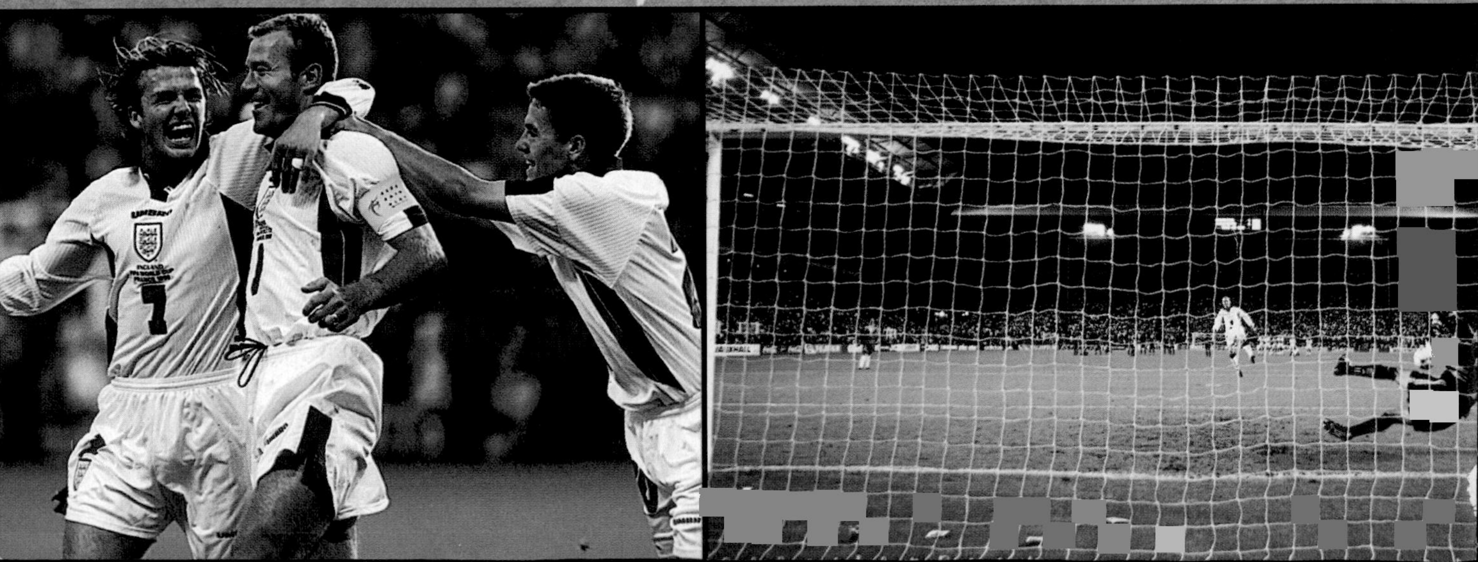

ROUND TWO ENGLAND v ARGENTINA

JUNE 30th 1998

ENGLAND 2-2 ARGENTINA (HT: 2-2)

[ARGENTINA WON 4-3 ON PENALTIES]

ENGLAND: Seaman, Campbell, Le Saux (sub: Southgate), Adams, Neville, Ince, Beckham, Anderton (sub: Batty), Scholes (sub: Merson), Shearer, Owen
Scorers: Shearer (10mins pen), Owen (16mins)
ARGENTINA: Roa, Ayala, Chamot, Vivas, Zanetti, Almeyda, Simeone (sub: Berti), Ortega, Veron, Lopez (sub: Gallardo), Batistuta (sub: Crespo)
Scorers: Batistuta (6mins pen), Zanetti (45mins)
REFEREE: K M Nielsen (Denmark)
ATT: 30,600 (Saint-Etienne)

A game of terrible bad luck for England and yet more penalty heartache to follow the spot-kick defeats by the Germans in 1990 and 1996. Glenn Hoddle's side began this second round game against their old Argentine rivals poorly, falling behind to a Gabriel Batistuta penalty after just six minutes when David Seaman brought down Diego Simeone.

Far from being downcast by the loss of such an early goal, however, England hit back within four minutes. Liverpool's Michael Owen, who'd made such an impact in barely quarter of an hour on the pitch against Romania, was upended in the penalty area by Roberto Ayala. Up stepped Alan Shearer to level the tie.

It was now that England enjoyed their best moments of the entire game and that dominance was down to one man – Owen. Every time he got hold of the ball the Argentinian defence hit the panic button. On 16 minutes he collected the ball well outside the opposition penalty area and roared towards goal, beating Ayala and Chamot as he went. Then, having looked like he might have taken the ball too wide to hit the target, the 18-year-old thumped his shot across the sprawling Roa into the net. 2-1 to England.

As half-time approached it looked likely that England would head off into the changing rooms a goal to the good. The ever inventive Argentinians had other ideas, however, and when Daniel Passarella's men won a free-kick just outside the English penalty box it was odds on that an equaliser was on its way. Zanetti slipped to one side of the England wall and, unmarked, received a clever pass, turned and slotted home past Seaman.

Despite the equaliser England still had every reason to believe they would progress to the Quarter-Finals, especially with Michael Owen threatening every time the ball fell at his feet. Sadly, we'll never know what might have been as the entire game turned on one unfortunate incident. David Beckham was fouled by Simeone barely two minutes after the restart and foolishly retaliated while he was lying on the floor. The kick earnt Beckham a red card and left Hoddle having to reorganise his 10-man side along more defensive lines. Even then Sol Campbell thought he'd won it for England but his header seven minutes from time was disallowed.

Extra time passed without serious incident (although England were denied a clear penalty when Chamot handled). And so to the shoot-out. Glenn Hoddle's men only had two regular spot-kickers left on the pitch – Owen and Shearer – and they, unsurprisingly, both found the net. Sadly, Paul Ince and David Batty, neither of whom are regular penalty takers, were also required to step up. This proved England's undoing and even though the Argentinians also missed a pen, Roa's save from Batty condemned England to an early exit. It was England's third penalty defeat in a major competition out of four and left an entire nation wondering when its luck was going to change.

ENGLAND'S MAN OF THE MATCH
SOL CAMPBELL

The Tottenham man had a brilliant World Cup and for many was probably the best defender in the tournament. He put in another commanding display against the Argentines, comfortable on the ball, calm under pressure and very unlucky to have what he thought was a winning goal disallowed for an Alan Shearer foul on 'keeper Roa. Had the goal stood Sol would have been a national hero, as it is he's still one of the country's most respected defenders and surely has a bright future at international level.

WORLD CUP '98

England and Scotland didn't make the Final but France and Brazil did – and what an incredible 90 minutes of shocks, surprises and terrific footie it was!

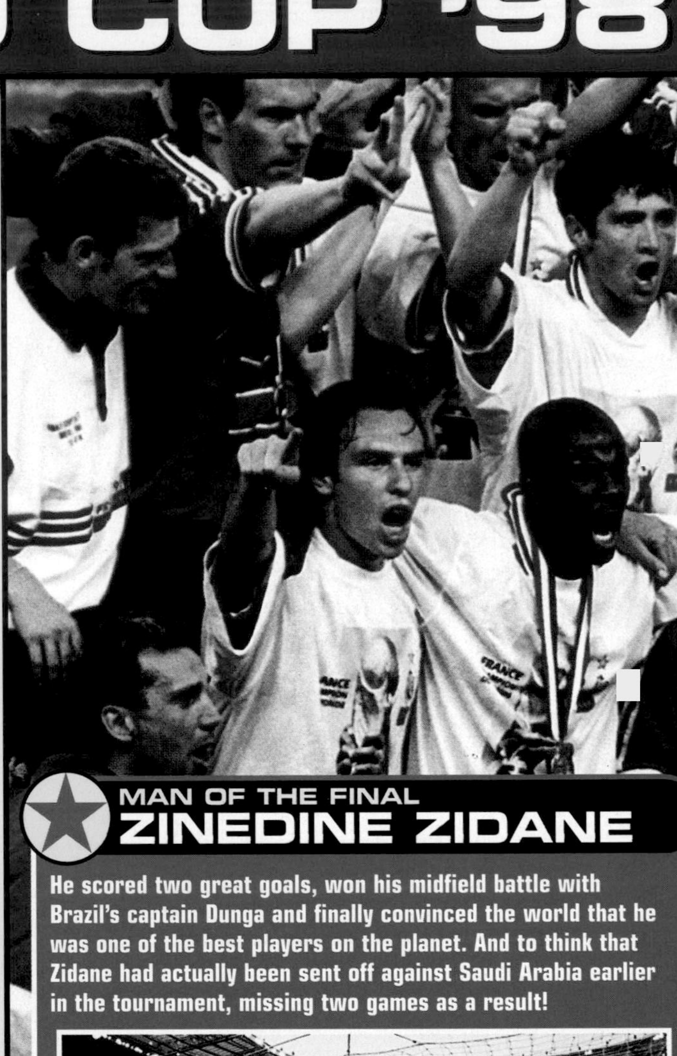

JULY 12th 1998

FRANCE 3-0 BRAZIL (HT: 2-0)

FRANCE: Barthez, Thuram, Leboeuf, Desailly, Lizarazu, Karembeu (sub: Boghossian), Deschamps, Petit, Zidane, Djorkaeff (sub: Vieira), Guivarc'h (sub: Dugarry)
Scorers: Zidane (27mins, 45mins), Petit (90mins)
BRAZIL: Taffarel, Cafu, Junior Baiano, Aldair, Roberto Carlos, Leonardo (sub: Denilson), Dunga, Cesar Sampaio (sub: Edmundo), Rivaldo, Ronaldo, Bebeto
REFEREE: S Belqola (Morocco)
ATT: 75,000 (Saint-Denis)

The drama in this Final had begun even before kick-off, when it transpired that Brazil coach Mario Zagallo had left Ronaldo out of the team because of injury. However, he quickly changed his mind when the world's best player declared himself fit and able to start the game after all. Unfortunately, Ronaldo's decision to play was a poor one and he looked a shadow of the star striker who'd threatened to set France '98 alight with four tournament goals and terrific displays against Holland and Chile. It later materialised that the Inter Milan star hadn't been injured at all but had been laid low by a mystery illness and had suffered convulsions. It was hardly the best of preparations for the Brazilians who didn't even appear before kick-off for their customary warm-up session.

Unsurprisingly, the samba men were very out of sorts and were lucky not to be two down inside four minutes when Newcastle's Stephane Guivarc'h spurned two excellent chances. The game continued in a similar pattern with the French always on top, while the Brazilians struggled to get the ball out of their own half. The breakthrough for the French came after 27 minutes when Inter Milan's Zinedine Zidane leaped to head home a fine corner from Emmanul Petit, with Brazil's defence all over the place.

On the stroke of half-time France made it 2-0 from a similiar move. This time a corner from the left was met by Zidane, who's low, bullet header thundered past 'keeper Taffarel. Brazil must have been mightily relieved when the half-time whistle went.

Despite his poor display Zagallo refused to substitute Ronaldo, instead swapping Leonardo for Denilson as the second half began. But despite the substitution and Brazil's keeness to pull an early goal back the French domination of the game continued. Only twice did the men in yellow seriously threaten Barthez. The first time the 'keeper needed to be at his best to smother a Ronaldo shot from point blank range, the second time Denilson hit the bar late on. It wasn't all plain sailing for France though, especially after they had Chelsea's Marcel Desailly sent off for a second bookable offence in the 68th minute. And yet, despite being reduced to ten men, there was never really any doubt that the French would hang on for a glorious victory to claim their first World Cup. Arsenal's Emmanuel Petit finished the rout of the former World Champs when he ran onto a fine pass from Dugarry to slot home past Taffarel making the final score 3-0 as the final whistle approached.

MAN OF THE FINAL
ZINEDINE ZIDANE

He scored two great goals, won his midfield battle with Brazil's captain Dunga and finally convinced the world that he was one of the best players on the planet. And to think that Zidane had actually been sent off against Saudi Arabia earlier in the tournament, missing two games as a result!

FINAL FRANCE v BRAZIL

UMBRO
17
UMBRO
17

ALL THE TOP INFO ON ALL YOUR FAVE STARS!

NO.1

MICHAEL OWEN

LIVERPOOL

ON HIS FIRST FOOTBALLING HERO

"Paul Gascoigne when he was playing in Italia '90 was my main hero when I was a youngster. When you get to play on the same pitch as your heroes it suddenly hits you. But after a few games you soon realise they're just like any normal footballer."

ON NERVES BEFORE A BIG GAME

"Obviously, I suffer from nerves slightly, but it doesn't really affect my game in any way. I tend not to get too tense before games, because I really look forward to them, but I do get excited about every match."

ON SCORING TEN MINUTES INTO HIS PROFESSIONAL CAREER

"It was a great achievement for me to score that goal against Wimbledon, but it was bad for the team that the game ended in defeat. We lost the Championship that night so everyone was really down afterwards."

ON HIS BIGGEST INFLUENCE

"Robbie Fowler and Steve McManaman. Watching them going through the ranks and showing the young lads that we can do it ourselves gave us all hope. We knew that if we were good enough that we'd be given the chance eventually."

ON THE ADULATION OF THE FANS

"I've always wanted to be a footballer and geared myself up for being one. A lot of people say it's an easy life, but there are other sides to the job that you've got to do that you might not enjoy so much. If people want your autograph, you've got to be prepared to give them your time."

ON TOUGH DEFENDERS

"I've taken a lot of punishment, but you just have to live with it. I'm playing against grown men who've been in the game for a long time, who know the different ways to handle a threat. The only thing you can do is stand up for yourself and answer them by sticking the ball in the back of the net."

ON HIS FUTURE IN THE GAME

"A lot of people have very high expectations of me, which I hope I can live up to. You see what happens to other players who start off with a bang and then fade away, but I'm confident enough to say that that shouldn't happen to me. I've got a feeling that it will never happen. I've got to keep on going and keep on scoring goals."

WHICH TEAM HE SUPPORTED AS A BOY

"I should keep this quiet, But I was an Everton fan just like Steve McManaman and Robbie Fowler!"

ON LIVERPOOL'S PREMIERSHIP CHANCES

"With the talent we have in our squad, I think we've as good a chance as any to win the League. Getting a good start is obviously important, but just as important is not to panic if you don't. We all realise there is a lot of pressure on us to do well in the league, and obviously doing well to Liverpool standards means winning the league or another major trophy. That brings the added pressure, but we are confident that we can cope."

ON HIS BEST FRIENDS AT ANFIELD

"The young lads who break into the team tend to stick together quite a lot. Danny Murphy is from around Chester like me, so we tend to hang around together."

ON HIS MAIN WEAKNESSES AS A PLAYER

"I've got to look at the defensive side of my game and defend from the front line. I work hard in training at that. I've got to follow in the footsteps of the great strikers who are defenders when the opposition have the ball."

CLASSIC CUP FINALS

FA CUP 1990
MAN UTD v C. PALACE

12TH MAY 1990:
MAN UTD 3- 3 C. PALACE (AET) (HT: 1-1)

C. PALACE: Martyn, Pemberton, Shaw, Gray, O'Reilly, Thorn, Barber (sub: Wright), Thomas, Bright, Salako (sub: Madden), Pardew. Scorers: O'Reilly, Wright (2)
MAN UTD: Leighton, Ince, Martin (sub: Blackmore), Bruce, Phelan, Pallister (sub: Robins), Robson, Webb, McClair, Hughes, Wallace. Scorers: Robson, Hughes (2)
REFEREE: A. Gunn (South Chailey)
ATT: 80,000 (At Wembley)

STAR MAN IAN WRIGHT

This fantastic Final saw a topsy-turvey game as honours ended even in front of a packed Wembley. Palace center-half Gary O'Reilly nodded 'The Eagles' ahead before Bryan Robson equalized for 'The Red Devils'. United took control and Mark Hughes smashed in a half-volley past Nigel Martyn. At this stage it looked like how many Manchester United would win by until Palace manager, Steve Coppell, made an inspired substitution and brought on Ian Wright. Within minutes Wrighty had scored a stunning solo goal and then swept Palace ahead in extra-time after a cross from wing wizard John Salako on the left.

However, Mark Hughes forced a replay with a deserved equalizer in a match which was a marvellous advert for the English game. In the replay five days later United full-back Lee Martin scored the only goal to give Alex Ferguson his first success as manager of Manchester United.

MOMENT OF THE MATCH

The inspired decision by Steve Coppell to replace Phil Barber with Ian Wright, who despite suffering from breaking a leg twice that season, single-handedly transformed what seemed a predictable Cup Final into a classic.

HOW THEY MADE THE FINAL

UNITED	PALACE
R3 v Nott'm Forest 1-0	R3 v Portsmouth 2-1
R4 v Hereford 1-0	R4 v Huddersfield 4-0
R5 v Newcastle 3-2	R5 v Rochdale 1-0
R6 v Sheff United 1-0	R6 v Cambridge 1-0
SF Oldham 3-3	SF v Liverpool 4-3
SF replay 2-1	

EVERYTHING YOU WANTED TO KNOW ABOUT

ASTON VILLA

If Arsenal are the kings of the south and Man United the kings of the north, then Aston Villa are without doubt the pride of the Midlands. Don't believe us? Then how come they've won seven league titles and FA Cups, plus two European trophies in the early 1980s? Yep, there's no doubt about it, Villa are one of the country's biggest sides. So if you want to know your Stan The Man from your Big Fat Ron, read on for the most comprehensive lowdown on the Villa Park giants you'll ever see!

FORMED: 1874
GROUND: Villa Park
NICKNAME: 'The Villans'
RECORD LEAGUE VICTORY: 12-2 v Accrington Stanley March 12th 1892.
MOST LEAGUE APPEARANCES: Charlie Aitken – 561 (1961-76).
MOST CAPPED PLAYER: Paul McGrath – 51 caps for Republic Of Ireland.
PLAYER WITH MOST LEAGUE GOALS: Harry Hampton – 215 league goals (1904-1915).
TOP SCORER 1997/98 (LEAGUE): Dwight Yorke 11

HONOURS: LEAGUE CHAMPIONS: 1893-94; 1895-96; 1896-97; 1898-99; 1899-1900; 1909-10; 1980-81. **F.A CUP:** 1887; 1895; 1897; 1905; 1913; 1920; 1957. **LEAGUE CUP:** 1961; 1975; 1977; 1994; 1996. **EUROPEAN CUP:** 1982. **EUROPEAN SUPER CUP WINNERS CUP:** 1983.

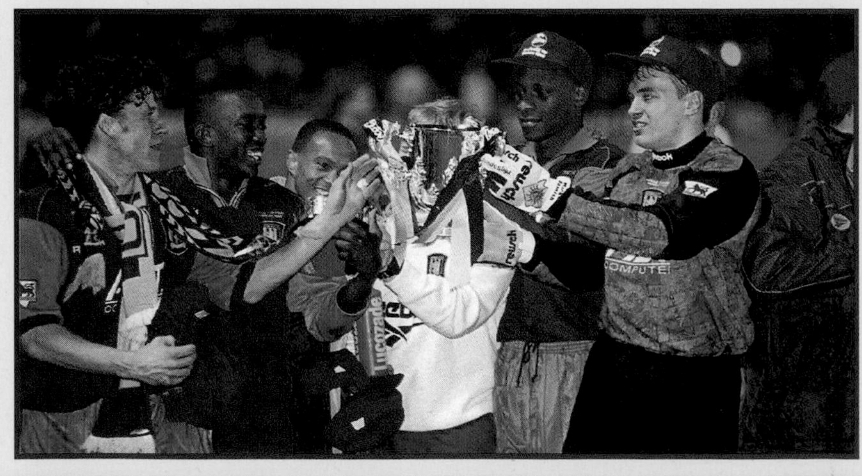

THE COUNTRY'S BIGGEST CLUBS!

GREAT MANAGER RON ATKINSON

'Big Ron' replaced Joseph Venglos in the Villa Park hot seat and his flamboyance rubbed off on the struggling side. He guided Villa to a League Cup success in 1994 against his former employers Man United. Always the colourful character, he is a popular figure.

WHAT A STAR VILLA'S GREAT PLAYERS

DAVID PLATT

Villa signed Platty for just £200,000 from Crewe Alexandra in 1988 – what a bargain he turned out to be! He became an England regular after scoring three goals at Italia '90. He scored 40 goals for the club from midfield and was sold to Italian Serie A side Bari in 1992 for a then British record £5.5million fee. Also appearing for Juventus and Sampdoria in Italy, he returned to England with Arsenal in 1995 and won the double there last season.

DWIGHT YORKE

Yorkie has been a consistent goalscorer for Villa since his arrival in 1991. He scored a stunning effort against Leeds in the 1996 Coca-Cola Cup Final and he is one of the most sought after players in England. Even Alex Ferguson was rumoured to be willing to break the Old Trafford bank to sign him! As if his goalscoring talents aren't enough, he can also set them up for his team-mates and he must be one of the happiest players around – he just can't stop smiling! He's also good mates with cricketer Brian Lara.

PAUL McGRATH

Remember the 'Ooh Aah, Cantona' chant? Well it actually started with Villa's former Irish defender Paul McGrath. As solid as they come, McGrath was a rock in the Villa defence between 1989 and 1996. A former Man United legend, McGrath's 'interesting' off the field activities meant he fell out with Alex Ferguson big time but he never had any problem with the Villa Park supporters. All together now: 'Ooh Aah, Paul McGrath!'

DID YOU KNOW?

James Major, son of former Prime Minister, John, had a trial with Aston Villa in 1990.

A-Z OF ENGLISH FOOTBALL

A is for AIR CRASH

The most infamous night in Man United's history happened on February 6th, 1958. The side was flying back from Yugoslavia having qualified for the European Cup Semi-Finals, but stopped in Munich, Germany so their plane could be refuelled in terrible conditions. Unable to take off again properly the plane ended up crashing into a house at the end of the runway. Twenty-three passengers were killed in the crash, including eight members of the legendary 'Busby Babes'.

B is for BANNED

In 1985 reigning European Champions Liverpool took on Italian giants Juventus in the Final of the European Cup at the Heysel Stadium in Brussels. Sadly, fighting broke out between the two sets of rival fans culminating in a wall collapsing. Nearly 40 people, mostly Italians, were crushed to death and another 400 injured. The terrible incident led to English teams being banned from all European competitions, a ruling that wasn't overturned until 1990.

C is for CHARITY SHIELD

The first Charity Shield was held in 1908 at Stamford Bridge and was contested between Man United, the league champions, and Queen's Park Rangers, the Southern league winners. The first game was drawn 1-1, but United won the replay 4-0. The more familiar FA Cup winners versus league champions format wasn't introduced until 1928, the match wasn't played before the start of the proper season until 1959 and Wembley wasn't used as its regular venue until 1974.

D is for DO I NOT LIKE THAT!

When Graham Taylor was appointed England boss after the 1990 World Cup practically everyone in the country greeted the decision warmly. After all, Taylor had been a successful club manager with Lincoln, Watford and Aston Villa, and seemed a natural choice to succeed Bobby Robson in the England hotseat. Unfortunately, it didn't all go to plan. Dumped embarrassingly out of Euro '92, England also failed to qualify for the World Cup in 1994. Taylor was eventually sacked but not before the newspapers gave him his infamous nickname – 'Turnip' – and he'd appeared in a hilarious TV documentary in which he infamously said, 'Do I Not Like That', during a World Cup qualification defeat by Holland. Now back in charge at Watford.

E is for EUROPEAN CUP

As difficult as it might now seem, there was a time when English clubs regularly won the European Cup. In fact, Liverpool, Nottingham Forest and Aston Villa once laid claim to the trophy seven times in just eight seasons back in the late '70s and early '80s. Unfortunately, such domination ended in 1984 and an English club hasn't won the trophy since.

F is for FOREIGN INVASION

Everyone knows the flash foreign likes of Vialli, Cantona, Schmeichel and Bergkamp, but stars from abroad have been present in the English game for years. Newcastle, for instance, had a Brazilian, Mirandinha, on their books in 1987 long before north-east rivals Middlesbrough snapped up Juninho and Emerson.

And what about Tottenham? In 1978 they signed Ossie Ardiles and Ricardo Villa, who'd starred for champions Argentina in the World Cup Finals of the same year. Liverpool, meanwhile, fielded an FA Cup Final winning team at Wembley in 1986 with only a single English born player in it – and he also qualified to play for the Republic Of Ireland!

G is for GREATEST SAVE OF ALL TIME

When England played Brazil in the World Cup Finals in 1970, 'keeper Gordon Banks made a save from Pele that has gone down as probably the most remarkable ever. The Brazilian Jairzinho had made an inch perfect cross into the English penalty area which Pele got on the end of at the far post with a downward bullet header. Amazingly, Banks, who had been covering the other goalpost at the time, threw himself right across the goal-line to somehow palm the ball away. Sadly, England went on to lose the match 1-0.

H is for HEARTBREAK

When it comes to heartbreak on the international stage nothing quite matches England's defeats to Germany in the 1990 World Cup and 1996's European Championship. Both matches were decided in the cruellest way possible – on penalties. In 1990 it was Stuart Pearce and Chris Waddle who missed the crucial spot-kicks, while in 1996, at Wembley, Aston Villa defender Gareth Southgate infamously had his pen saved by German 'keeper Kopke. No-one could have believed it would all happen again against Argentina last summer.

I is for INJURY TIME WINNER

The most exciting finale to a football league season ever came in 1989 when Liverpool and Arsenal were equal on points at the top of the table with just one game left to play – against each other! In fact, the Merseyside outfit only needed to avoid defeat at Anfield by two goals to be crowned league champions. 'The Gunners' took the lead in the game early in the second half but as the minutes ticked by it looked more and more likely that Liverpool would hang on. Then, deep into injury time, Arsenal midfielder Michael Thomas powered through to score 'The Gunners'' second with the last kick of the game. Amazing – but not if you were a Liverpool fan!

J is for JUST ANOTHER FEW MINUTES

Extra time has been a part of the English game since way back in 1875 when the Royal Engineers and Old Etonians clashed in the FA Cup Final. The result that day was 1-1 and the game had to be decided after a replay. Although the limit on playing extra-time has for the most part been two halves of 15 minutes the rule book went out of the window in 1946 when Stockport and Doncaster met in the FA Cup and a result had to be reached that day. The game went on for 203 minutes (over three hours) and was eventually only stopped because of bad light with the score at 4-4!

K is for KUNG-FU KICK

When Eric Cantona joined Leeds United in 1992 no-one could quite have imagined the impact this fiery French import would have on the English game. He was one of the main reasons why the Yorkshire side marched to the title in the same season even though he'd only been an Elland Road regular for a few months. Astonishingly, Leeds opted to sell Cantona early the following season to arch rivals Man United. His impact at Old Trafford was even more marked, inspiring them to the Championship in his first season and the double the year after that. However, if there's one incident Monsicur Cantona will be remembered for it is his kung-fu kick assault on an abusive fan at Crystal Palace in January 1995. Eric The Red received a nine month ban for the incident, in which United lost their title to Blackburn and were defeated in the FA Cup Final by Everton.

L is for LEAGUE TITLES

Although Arsenal are the current top-flight champs and Man United have won the title four times in six seasons, it's Liverpool who have won the most championships. 'The Reds' first won the title back in 1901 and have since added another 17 league championships to their trophy cabinet. Arsenal and Man United are second in the most league titles stakes with 11, while Everton have won nine.

A-Z OF ENGLISH FOOTBALL

M is for MILLION POUND MAN

Long before he was manager of Birmingham City, Trevor Francis was the country's most expensive player. Francis had started his career with 'The Blues' at 16 and went on to score 118 goals in 278 appearances. In 1979 he was snapped up by ambitious Nottingham Forest for £1.15million, more than doubling the previous record for a British transfer. Francis repaid Forest's faith by scoring the winning goal in that season's European Cup Final.

N is for NEAR AND YET SO FAR

In the 1995-96 season Newcastle United, under manager Kevin Keegan, seemed set to win the Premiership. They led the table almost from the first day of the season and, at one point, were 12 points clear of nearest rivals Man United. Astonishingly, the wheels fell off Toon's championship bandwagon. They lost their unbeaten home record to United at the beginning of March and simply couldn't get it together after that, losing dramatically to both Liverpool and Blackburn. Toon could only draw their final two games of the season, as United won 13 of their last 15 to clinch the title comfortably.

O is for OLD INVINCIBLES

The nickname given to Preston, who dominated English football in its early days. The Lancashire side won the very first league championship by 11 points without losing a game and were also FA Cup winners in the same season. Preston were also the first club to pay players for their services.

P is for PREMIERSHIP

Although there's been an English top-flight for the last 110 years the Premier League didn't actually come into being until 1992. Manchester United became the first club to lift the trophy and in doing so claimed their only championship success since 1967. To prove it wasn't a fluke 'The Red Devils' went on to win the Prem another three times over the next five years.

Q is for QUALITY

According to some English football is no longer the best in the world, but every now and again a player is born on these shores who takes the world by storm. Bobby Moore, who captained England to World Cup glory in 1966 and is rated by Pele as the best defender of all-time, Paul Gascoigne, who with better luck could have become the best player on the planet and former England striker Gary Lineker. Lineker started his career with Leicester City, helping them win promotion as champions from the old Second Division in 1978. His formidable reputation, including a 26 goal haul in 1983, saw him called up by England for the first time in 1984 and transfered to Everton in 1985. In 1986 he won two Player Of The Year awards, scored 30 league goals and his six strikes in the World Cup Finals landed him the prestigious Golden Boot.

R is for RIGHT HAMMERINGS!

It's always a nightmare to see your team beaten – but it's even worse when the opposition runs riot and scores five, six, seven or more. Man United hold the record for the biggest margin of victory in the Premiership, they stuffed sorry Ipswich 9-0 in 1995. But that has nothing on the scale of Preston's win over Hyde United in the FA Cup way back in 1887. The Lancashire side ran out winners by 26 goals to nil!

S is for SCOTTISH MANAGERS

The last English manager to win the English league championship was Howard Wilkinson – in 1992. In fact the most successful bosses in English footie over the last 15 years have been Scots, winning ten titles in that time, including five on the trot between 1993 and 1997. Man United's Alex Ferguson and Kenny Dalglish are the most successful Scottish bosses, weighing in with four titles each, although Dalglish did it with two clubs – Liverpool and Blackburn. George Graham is the other top Scot with two titles in his time at Arsenal.

T is for THEY THINK IT'S ALL OVER... IT IS NOW!

"There's some people on the pitch. They think it's all over... it is now!" is the most famous line of TV football commentary ever and came at the end of England's World Cup Final victory over West Germany in 1966. England, already leading 3-2 in extra-time, were just seconds from victory when striker Geoff Hurst collected the ball and headed like an express train towards the German goal. Just as he prepared to lash the ball into the net commentator Kenneth Wolstenholme noticed that some England fans had already made it onto the Wembley pitch to start celebrating an historic win. However, before he could comment further Hurst banged the ball past 'keeper Tikowski to make it 4-2.

U is for UNBELIEVABLE!

English football history is littered with upsets and surprises – the day fourth division Colchester knocked the mighty Leeds out of the FA Cup in 1971 or when non-League Hereford ejected Arsenal from the same competition the following season. But no football giantkilling act comes close to matching the day in 1950 when, in a World Cup match in Brazil, the United States beat England 1-0. At the time it was an utterly unthinkable result as England were considered one of the best sides in the world. In fact, when the result was announced in England some newspapers thought it was a typing error and changed it to 10-1 to England!

V is for VIOLENCE

English fans have a reputation throughout the world for being trouble-makers. It is a belief reinforced by the appalling actions of England fans during last summer's World Cup Finals in France when dozens were arrested during violent clashes with riot police. However, violence amongst English fans isn't anything new. English clubs were banned from Europe following the actions of Liverpool fans at 1985's European Cup Final, while 1988's European Championships in Germany saw almost 400 England supporters detained by police. Probably the worst football hooliganism seen on English soil, however, came during the 1984-85 season when Millwall fans staged a pitched battle with 200 police officers at Luton following an FA Cup Quarter-Final. Unsurprisingly, Luton banned away fans from their ground altogether just a few seasons later.

W is for WEMBLEY

Originally called the Empire Stadium, Wembley was built in 300 days for £750,000 just in time for the 1923 FA Cup Final between Bolton and West Ham. Over 200,000 spectators turned up for that game even though the stadium was only supposed to house 127,000! In fact, there were so many in the stadium that day the crowd actually spilled out of the terraces onto the pitch and mounted policemen struggled to maintain order. The first international game to be staged at Wembley followed the year after when England drew 1-1 with Scotland. Wembley will be closed after the 1999 FA Cup Final for the most major refurbishment in its history as it bids to become the most impressive sporting stadium in the world.

X is for XTRAORDINARY!

English footie is awash with amazing records and record breakers. Former England 'keeper Peter Shilton, for instance, holds the record for the highest number of appearances in the English league. He clocked up 1005 with eight different clubs between 1966 and 1997. Then there's Everton's Dixie Dean. He holds the record for the highest number of league goals in a season – 60 for Everton back in 1927-28 in just 39 games. Dean also holds the record for the highest number of hat-tricks in a career – 34.

Y is for YOUNG GUNS

When Liverpool's Michael Owen came on as a substitute in the friendly against Chile at Wembley in February 1998 he became the youngest player to pull on an England shirt this century. But at 18 years and 59 days old he certainly isn't the youngest record breaker in the English game. Former West Ham 'keeper, Neil Finn, for instance, is the youngest player to ever appear in the Premiership at just 17 years and three days, while Tottenham's Andy Turner became the Prem's youngest scorer when he netted against Everton in 1992 aged just 17 years, 166 days. Alan Shearer, meanwhile, is the youngest player to ever score a top-flight hat-trick. He put three past Arsenal for Southampton in 1988 when he was 17 years, 240 days old.

Z is for ZERO

The number of major trophies won by Middlesbrough FC. The Teesiders are the only Premiership club never to have won the Championship, the FA Cup or the League Cup.

ALL THE TOP INFO ON ALL YOUR FAVE STARS!

NO.2 PAUL MERSON

ON HIS FAVOURITE MANAGERS

"It was George Graham who gave me my chance at Arsenal. He would give you a right telling off when you needed it. He always had a positive approach to everything, despite what some people used to say. Arsene Wenger? I can't speak highly enough of him. He's a great tactician and knows about man-management. He is also very positive, and you know where you stand with him. I always admired Bryan Robson as a player, so naturally I jumped at the chance to join him at Boro."

ON THE QUALITY OF THE PREMIERSHIP

"I think it's probably the best league in the world, certainly entertainment wise. I think the young players are benefitting from playing alongside the top foreigners. The league's getting harder, but that's the way it should be."

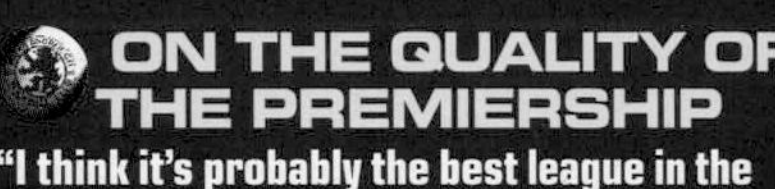

ON SIGNING UP FOR BORO

"Bryan Robson being manager had a lot to do with me joining. I never wanted to leave Arsenal – it was a bolt out of the blue. It never occurred to me that Arsene Wenger would sell me, although as soon as I heard about Middlesborough's interest I said 'yes' straight away. They're a big club without a doubt, and looking to go forward."

ON BEING SOLD BY 'THE GUNNERS'

"Many of the players were sad to see me go, but they were pleased for me as well. I'm so glad they went on and won the championship – I've still got a lot of friends there. But that is all in the past – I'm a Middlesborough player now, and that is all that concerns me. It'd be nice to put one over them in the Premiership though!"

ON PLAYING AT WEMBLEY

"It really is as good as everyone makes it out to be, and everytime I'm due to play I can't wait to get out there. There are loads of great grounds in England like the Riverside, Highbury and Old Trafford, but to play at Wembley is the pinnacle for anyone in the game."

ON SETTLING DOWN ON TEESIDE

"The best thing about being a player for Middlesbrough is the fans – they have really surprised me with the passion they have shown. They are the best fans in the world – they've made it easy for me to settle down in the area."

ON BORO'S SUCCESS LAST SEASON

"It's turned into such a massive club, so we do expect to be challenging for all the top honours. Promotion last season was obviously the main concern for us and I would expect us to do well again this year in the Premiership."

ON HIS RETURN TO THE INTERNATIONAL STAGE WITH ENGLAND

"It certainly wasn't something I considered a couple of years back when I wasn't even sure I had a future in the game. I thought my time with England might have passed me by. It just shows you should never give up."

ON PLAYING IN THE FIRST DIVISION

"It was the first time that I had played at that level, so it was a bit of a culture shock really. I'm glad we made the automatic promotion place, because I don't think I could have played one more game. I was shattered – 46 games plus a cup run takes a lot from you. It was a lot harder than I ever imagined it would be, because it's like a cup final for practically every team you play."

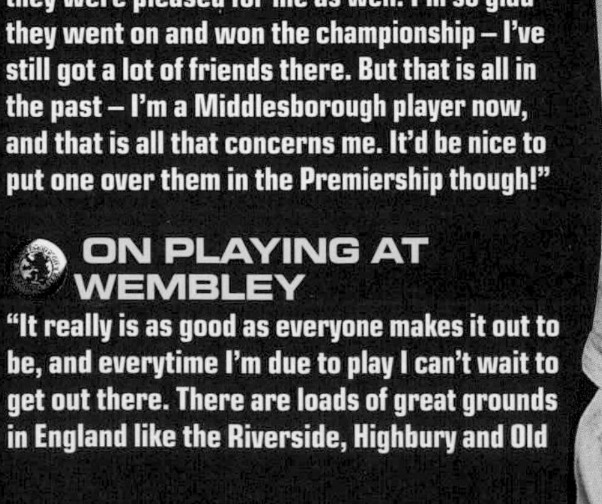

errea
Cellnet

CLASSIC CUP FINALS

FA CUP 1989
LIVERPOOL v EVERTON

MAY 20th 1989

LIVERPOOL 3-2 EVERTON (AET) (HT: 1-0)

LIVERPOOL: Grobbelaar, Ablett, Staunton (sub: Venison), Nicol, Whelan, Hansen, Beardsley, Aldridge (sub: Rush), Houghton, Barnes, McMahon. Scorers: Aldridge, Rush (2)
EVERTON: Southall, McDonald, Van Den Hauwe, Ratcliffe, Watson, Bracewell (sub: McCall), Nevin, Steven, Sharp, Cottee, Sheedy (sub: Wilson). Scorers: McCall (2)
REFEREE: J. Worrall (Warrington).
ATT: 82,800 (At Wembley)

STAR MAN IAN RUSH

Supersub Ian Rush proved that lightning does strikes twice when he repeated his two-goal salvo from the 1986 Cup Final against Everton. 'The Reds" John Aldridge scored with his first touch to banish his personal Wembley nightmare after his penalty miss against Wimbledon a year earlier. And it appeared that Aldo was going to be the match-winner until Everton sub Stuart McCall stabbed in an equalizer. Rushie put 'Pool back in front five minutes into extra-time before that tartan terror McCall volleyed a superb second equalizer.

However, Rushie had the last word when he nodded past his Welsh International team-mate Neville Southall to beat Dixie Dean's record of 19 goals in Merseyside derbies. The magnificent game in the Wembley sunshine boosted the area of Merseyside following that year's Hillsborough tragedy.

MOMENT OF THE MATCH

Rush showed he had lost none of his predatory skills by controlling a centre from Nicol, turning Ratcliffe beautifully and driving the ball into the far-corner of the goal to put Liverpool 2-1 ahead in extra time.

HOW THEY MADE THE FINAL

LIVERPOOL	EVERTON
R3 v Carlisle 3-0	R3 v West Brom 1-1
R4 v Millwall 2-0	R3 replay v West Brom 1-0
R5 v Hull 3-2	R4 v Plymouth 1-1
R6 v Brentford 4-0	R4 replay v Plymouth 4-0
SF v Nott'm Forest 3-1	R5 v Barnsley 1-0
	R6 v Wimbledon 1-0
	SF v Norwich 1-0

EVERYTHING YOU WANTED TO KNOW ABOUT

RANGERS

Last season was a strange one for Rangers – they didn't win anything. Such has been the Glasgow giants' domination of the Scottish game in recent years, a season without at least one trophy on the sideboard is considered a disaster and when you look at the history and traditions of the club, you can see why! With a new manager, Dutchman Dick Advocaat, in charge, they are expected to re-emerge with a vengence this season. Read all about Gers' past glories in SHOOT's comprehensive guide.

FORMED: 1873
GROUND: Ibrox Stadium
NICKNAME: 'The Gers'
RECORD VICTORY: 14-2 v Blairgowrie January 20th 1934.
MOST LEAGUE APPEARANCES: John Grieg – 496 appearances (1962-78).
MOST CAPPED PLAYER: Ally McCoist – 58 Caps for Scotland (1996-97).
RECORD GOALSCORER: Ally McCoist – 244 (1985-98)
PLAYER WITH MOST LEAGUE GOALS: Ally McCoist – 254 (1985-98).
TOP SCORER 1997/98 (LEAGUE): Marco Negri 32

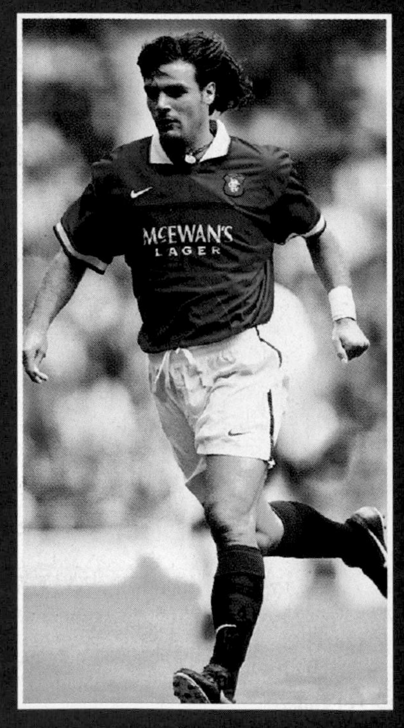

HONOURS: SCOTTISH LEAGUE CHAMPIONS: 1890- 91 (shared); 1898-99; 1899-00; 1900-01; 1901-02; 1910-11; 1911-12; 1912-13; 1917-18; 1919-20; 1920-21; 1922-23; 1923-24; 1924-25; 1926-27; 1927-28; 1928-29; 1929-30; 1930-31; 1932-33; 1933-34; 1934-35; 1936-37; 1938-39; 1946-47; 1948-49; 1949-50; 1952-53; 1955-56; 1956-57; 1958-59; 1960-61; 1962-63; 1963-64; 1974-75; 1975-76; 1977-78; 1986-87; 1988-89; 1989-90; 1990-91; 1991-1992; 1992-93; 1993-94; 1994-95; 1995-96; 1996-97. **SCOTTISH CUP:** 1894; 1897; 1898; 1903; 1928; 1930; 1932; 1934; 1935; 1936; 1948; 1950; 1953; 1960; 1962; 1963; 1964; 1966; 1973; 1976; 1978; 1979; 1981; 1992; 1993; 1996. **SCOTTISH LEAGUE CUP:** 1947; 1949; 1961; 1962; 1964; 1965; 1971; 1976; 1978; 1979; 1982; 1984; 1985; 1987; 1988; 1989; 1991.

THE COUNTRY'S BIGGEST CLUBS!

GREAT MANAGER WALTER SMITH

Smith was one of the most influential managers in Scottish footballing history. He led Rangers to seven consecutive League titles, three League cups and three Scottish Cups. Even though his final season at the club ended trophyless, he will never be forgotten.

WHAT A STAR RANGERS' GREAT PLAYERS

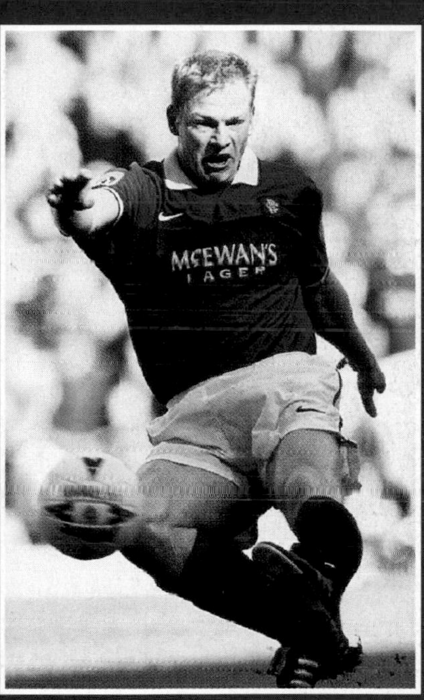

ALLY McCOIST

As a teenager Ally was considered too small to be a centre-forward! He has responded by becoming one of the most prolific goalscorers in modern football. His 34 goals in 1992 earned him the Golden Boot award as Europe's leading marksman. Even at 35 years of age he shows no sign of letting opposition defences rest in peace and he signed off from 'The Gers' with a goal in last season's Scottish Cup Final. One of club's greatest ever goalscorers.

RICHARD GOUGH

The Swedish born defender has returned to Ibrox after a short spell in America. He was signed from Tottenham in 1987 and Gough's professionalism and desire to win saw Rangers grab their ninth title in a row. He won the Scottish Player Of The Year award In 1989. In his first game back for Rangers he scored the only goal in the Old Firm derby at Ibrox, and shows no sign of losing the competitiveness and courage that have become the hallmark of his game at club and international level.

JORG ALBERTZ

Jorg Albertz has become the heart of the Glasgow Rangers midfield – and Gers supporters will be hoping he becomes the heart of the Rangers revival. A strong competitive player, the German international arrived from Hamburger SV – and immediately showed he had a massive appetitie for success by scoring 10 goals from the middle of the park in his first season at Ibrox. A born winner, he could be the club's lynchpin for years to come.

DID YOU KNOW?

Manchester United boss Alex Ferguson played in a Scottish Cup Final for Rangers.

CHAMPIONS

ARSENAL
PREMIERSHIP CHAMPIONS & FA CUP WINNERS

In only his first full season in charge at Highbury French boss Arsene Wenger delivered Arsenal's second league and cup double in dramatic circumstances.

No-one would have thought 'The Gunners' capable of winning anything at one point in the season, as their league form faltered and arch rivals Man United seemed destined to run away with the honours yet again. But Arsenal made an incredible recovery in the Premiership, going almost five months without defeat and beating United at Old Trafford. In the end, Wenger's men, who included Player Of The Year Dennis Bergkamp, French whizzkid Nicolas Anelka and flying Dutchman Marc Overmars, won the title with two games to spare. It was their first Championship since 1991.

However, the icing on the cake for Gunners fans came at Wembley in the FA Cup Final. Up against Kenny Dalglish's Newcastle, who'd had a poor season by their standards, Tony Adams, Martin Keown and co put on a virtuoso performance. Goals from Marc Overmars and Nicolas Anelka settled the tie and broke Geordie hearts in the process. Arsenal's trophy haul meant they'd become only the second team in English history to win the double twice.

'98 MEET THE TEAMS WHO TOOK THE TOP TROPHIES AT HOME AND ABROAD LAST SEASON!

CHELSEA
COCA-COLA CUP & EUROPEAN CUP WINNERS' CUP WINNERS

It was a clean sweep of domestic trophies for London as Gianluca Vialli's side won the Coca-Cola Cup at Wembley against Middlesbrough. It was the second time in less than a year that the two sides had come face to face in a major Wembley Final – and the result was the same again – 2-0 to Chelsea.

Not that 'The Blues' had had an easy route to Wembley. They'd beaten Blackburn and Ipswich on penalties and were taken to extra-time by Southampton. Then there was that titantic Semi-Final struggle with Arsenal, who led 2-1 from the first leg at Highbury. Goals from Mark Hughes, Roberto Di Matteo and Dan Petrescu settled the tie at Stamford Bridge.

Chelsea had only won a European trophy once before – back in 1971 when they'd defeated Real Madrid in the Cup Winners' Cup. It was fitting then that the same competition should give 'The Blues' their second European success.

Again their passage to the Final was tough – losing 3-2 to Norwegians Tromso in arctic conditions and trailing Vicenza 2-0 in the Semi-Final games. But Vialli's men came through and it was Italian substitute Gianfranco Zola who struck their winner against VFB Stuttgart of Germany. The ex-Parma striker had been on the pitch less than a minute when he picked up a Dennis Wise pass to fire Chelsea back into the big time!

CELTIC

SCOTTISH PREMIER LEAGUE CHAMPIONS & SCOTTISH COCA-COLA CUP WINNERS

It was all change in Scotland last season as Rangers' dominance was finally broken. Celtic, desperate to stop their rivals claiming ten Championship victories in a row, got off to a slow start in the Premier League with two defeats against unfancied Hibernian and Dunfermline. But Dutch manager Wim Jansen soon whipped 'The Bhoys' into shape, as Walter Smith's men failed to get their act together, despite several high profile, big money signings.

Celtic clinched their first Scottish Championship since 1988 on the last day of the season in a 2-0 win over St Johnstone. 'The Bhoys" victory celebrations were to turn sour, however, as Jansen resigned following an ongoing dispute with the Celtic board.

Before winning their 36th title, Celtic had managed to reacquaint themselves with another trophy they hadn't seen for awhile – the Scottish Coca-Cola Cup. The last time the Glasgow giants had won the tournament was way back in 1983 and they'd been beaten finalists four times since then, including an embarrassing penalties defeat by Raith in 1995. But this time 'The Bhoys' made no slip ups, cruising to a 3-0 win over Dundee United at Ibrox thanks to goals from Marc Rieper, Henrik Larsson and Scottish Player Of The Year Craig Burley. All in all a terrific return to form.

REAL MADRID

EUROPEAN CUP WINNERS

Few would have given Spanish side Real Madrid much chance of beating mighty Italian outfit Juventus in the Champions League Final in Amsterdam. After all Real had had a poor season in their domestic league, only finishing fourth behind Athletic Bilbao and Real Sociedad, as bitter rivals Barcelona took top spot. Juventus, meanwhile, had eased to yet another Italian title and boasted the likes of Del Piero, Inzaghi and Zidane amongst their star studded ranks. However, the form book was turned inside out and upside down as Juve crashed to their second Champions League Final defeat in succession thanks to a goal from Yugoslav international Pedrag Mijatovic after 67 minutes.

HEARTS
SCOTTISH FA CUP WINNERS

It was a terrific season for Hearts. Not only had they been a good outside bet to nick the title off Rangers for most of the season but they also managed a famous victory over Walter Smith's much fancied side in the Scottish FA Cup Final at Parkhead. 'The Jambos' were chasing their first trophy in 42 years and got off to the best possible start when they were awarded a controversial penalty in the first minute of the game which Colin Cameron converted. Despite an excellent display by Denmark international and now Chelsea star Brian Laudrup, the Glasgow side just couldn't find a way back into the game and fell further behind when Frenchman Stephane Adam rifled Hearts into an uncatchable two goal lead early in the second half. Despite an Ally McCoist consolation with nine minutes left, Walter Smith's last game in charge of Rangers had ended in defeat and his final season trophyless. Hearts, meanwhile, celebrated a glorious victory and the chance of European football come the new season.

INTER MILAN
UEFA CUP WINNERS

As their city rivals AC Milan stumbled from crisis to crisis Inter slowly but surely became the main challenger to Juventus' total domination of Italian football. First they signed the Brazilian Ronaldo, arguably the world's best player, and then they won their first European trophy since 1991. In truth, coach Simoni's men hardly needed to work up a sweat to overcome a clearly outclassed Lazio outfit who were a goal down and in trouble after barely five minutes. It came as no surprise when the Argentine Zanetti doubled Inter's lead 15 minutes after the restart and Ronaldo rounded off a resounding victory. Even the sending off of Inter's Nigerian defender Taribo West couldn't take the gloss off a wonderful night for the Italian giants.

JVC

ALL THE TOP INFO ON ALL YOUR FAVE STARS!

NO.3

MARC OVERMARS

ARSENAL

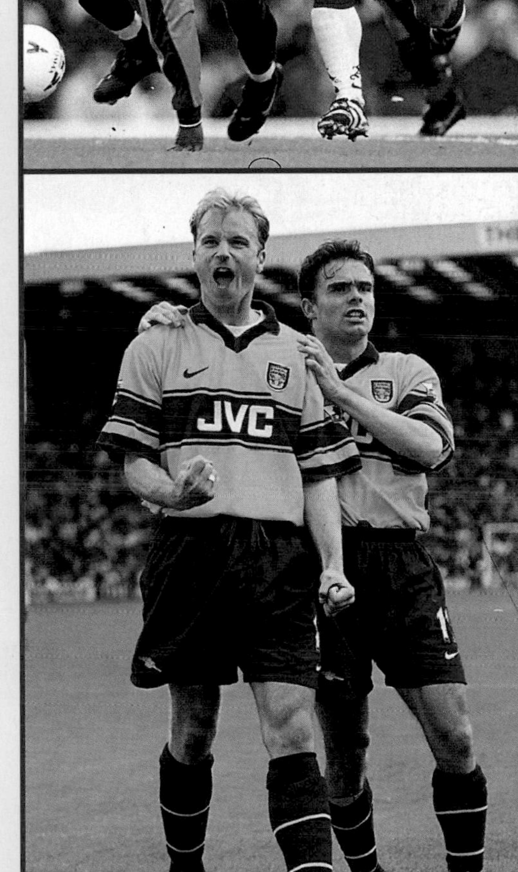

ON PLAYING IN THE PREMIERSHIP

"It is a different kind of football here to the one that I was used to in Holland. There is always something going on throughout the whole 90 minutes of each game."

ON PLAYING IN THE CHAMPIONS LEAGUE

"It's so important for a club like Arsenal to be winning trophies, and of course to be in the Champions League. I'm so happy to be playing in that competition again. It's great to win on a domestic level, but we have to show how good we are on a European stage."

ON PLAYING ALONGSIDE DENNIS BERGKAMP

"He was a friend of mine from my time at Ajax and the Holland team, so it was an extra encouragement for me to join Arsenal. He is a great individual player but he is also a very supportive team player, which I think is very important. He is such a complete footballer."

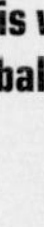

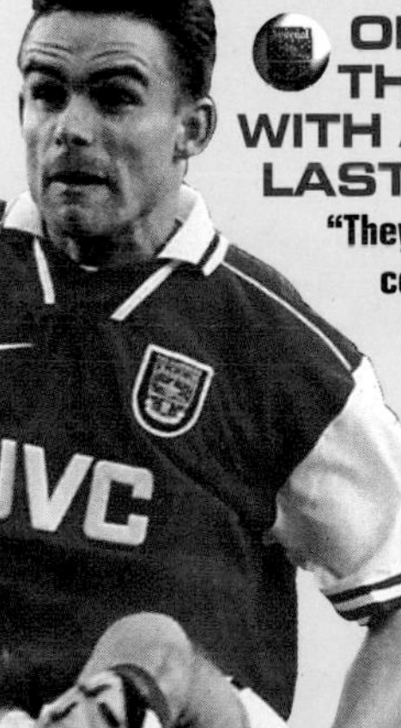

ON ENGLISH SUPPORTERS

"I have had a good reaction from them. They are louder than the Dutch, that's for sure. You can feel the enthusiasm here more. Fans in this country are more passionate than in Holland and that is good for the players. A good atmosphere can really lift the players."

ON LEAVING AJAX

"It wasn't easy to go because they are a great club who have won many prizes. I made the right choice by coming to Arsenal – to win the double in my first season here was fantastic."

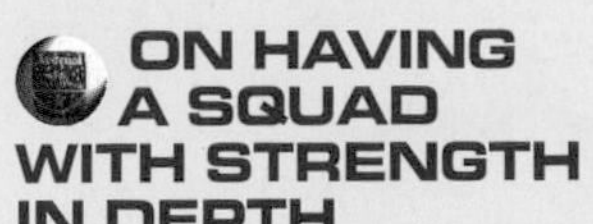

ON HAVING A SQUAD WITH STRENGTH IN DEPTH

"It's essential that we have a good squad for the manager to pick from, especially in Europe. In my last year at Ajax we didn't have that, whereas in the years before that we had a whole squad of good players. But good players never want to sit on the bench as substitutes, that is the problem."

ON PLAYING IN LONDON DERBIES

"London derbies are always very intense affairs, and all the players get really hyped up about them beforehand. It's good fun, and it's not very far to travel – also for the fans it's more interesting when we play against the likes of Spurs or Chelsea. In Holland we only have a few matches like that. We have Ajax and Feyenoord, but that's not a derby like the ones over here."

ON GETTING SERIOUSLY INJURED

"I was out for seven months at Ajax with an injury to my left knee. But I am now just as quick as I was before. It just takes a long time for some injuries to heal. Despite what some people said, there was never any question of it ending my career."

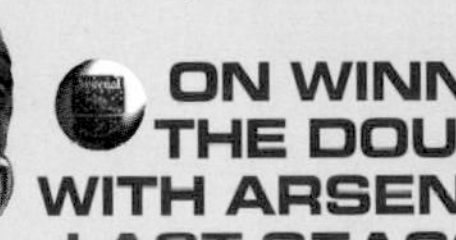

ON WINNING THE DOUBLE WITH ARSENAL LAST SEASON

"They're both such great competitions, and I'm so proud to have won them with Arsenal. There are so many good teams in England and that makes it all the more of an achievement."

ON JAAP STAM, MAN UNITED'S NEW DUTCHMAN

"I think Jaap has brought a lot of pace to the United defence and he's taken a lot of pressure off their other defensive players. He's showed he can handle quality opponents in the World Cup and has done the same in the Premiership. As well as being fast, he's also very strong and he likes to play simple football. I think he was a very good buy for United even at £10.5 million."

CLASSIC CUP FINALS

FA CUP 1994

MAN UTD v CHELSEA

14TH MAY 1994: MAN UTD 4-0 CHELSEA (HT: 0-0)

MAN UTD: Schmeichel, Parker, Irwin (sub: Sharpe), Bruce, Kanchelskis (sub: McClair), Pallister, Cantona, Ince, Keane, Hughes, Giggs. Scorers: Cantona (2), Hughes, McClair
CHELSEA: Kharine, Clarke, Sinclair, Kjeldbjerg, Johnsen, Burley (sub: Hoddle), Spencer, Newton, Stein (sub: Cascarino), Peacock, Wise.
REFEREE: D.Elleray (Harrow)
ATT: 79,634 (At Wembley)

STAR MAN ERIC CANTONA

United made history by becoming only the fourth club this century to complete the League and FA Cup double. They gained sweet revenge on 'The Blues' who were the only team to beat them twice in the League that season. The PFA Footballer Of The year Eric Cantona put United ahead from the penalty spot on the hour.

The Frenchman repeated the trick six minutes later when Frank Sinclair was harshly adjudged to have fouled Andrei Kanchelskis in the box. Mark Hughes scored his fourth Wembley goal shortly after and even the appearance of Chelsea player-manager Glenn Hoddle failed to galvanize the west Londoners as Brian McClair completed the scoring.

MOMENT OF THE MATCH

Eric Cantona, the King Of Old Trafford, broke the deadlock on the hour with an ice-cool penalty to set Man United on the road to their first League and Cup Double.

HOW THEY MADE THE FINAL

CHELSEA	UNITED
R3 v Barnet 0-0	R3 v Sheff United 1-0
R3 replay v Barnet 4-0	R4 v Norwich 2-0
R4 v Sheff Wed 1 1	R5 v Wimbledon 3-0
R4 replay v Sheff Wed 3-1	R6 v Charlton 3-1
R5 v Oxford 2-1	SF v Oldham 1-1
R6 v Wolves 1-0	SF replay v Oldham 4-1
SF v Luton 2-0	

EVERYTHING YOU WANTED TO KNOW ABOUT

TOTTENHAM

They may have lived in the shadows of London rivals Arsenal and Chelsea in recent years, but Tottenham have a proud history of glory. Before the likes of Sol Campbell were even born, they were celebrating the double in 1961 and have gone on some famous cup runs in their time. Then came the silky skills of players such as Glenn Hoddle, Chris Waddle and Paul Gascoigne. SHOOT's got the full lowdown on the White Hart Lane side, so if you're mad about Spurs, read on!

FORMED: 1882
GROUND: White Hart Lane
NICKNAME: 'Spurs'
RECORD LEAGUE VICTORY: 9-0 v Bristol Rovers October 22nd 1977.
MOST LEAGUE APPEARANCES: Steve Perryman – 655 appearances (1969-86).
MOST CAPPED PLAYER: Pat Jennings – 74 caps for Northern Ireland.
PLAYER WITH MOST LEAGUE GOALS: Jimmy Greaves – 220 goals (1961-1970).
TOP SCORER 1997/98 (LEAGUE): Jurgen Klinsmann 9

HONOURS: LEAGUE CHAMPIONSHIPS: 1950-51; 1960-61. **F.A CUP:** 1901; 1921; 1961; 1962; 1967; 1981; 1982; 1991. **LEAGUE & FA CUP DOUBLE:** 1961. **LEAGUE CUP:** 1971; 1973. **EUROPEAN CUP WINNERS CUP:** 1963. **UEFA CUP:** 1972; 1984.

GREAT MANAGER TERRY VENABLES

'El Tel' became Spurs boss In 1987 and made exciting signings such as Paul Gascoigne and Gary Lineker. His teams played with flair and distinction and he was rewarded with the FA Cup in 1991, after overcoming rivals Arsenal in style in the Semi-Final at Wembley.

WHAT A STAR TOTTENHAM'S GREAT PLAYERS

GLENN HODDLE

The midfield genius was nicknamed 'The King of White Hart Lane', and if you've seen any of his goals, you'll know why! He joined Spurs from school and made his debut in August 1975. Before long, his breathtaking skills and spectacular goals helped Tottenham win the FA Cup in 1981 and 1982. Now the England boss, the attractive style played by the national side mirrors perfectly the grace and skill he showed off week after week at White Hart Lane. A true legend!

PAUL GASCOIGNE

"Up steps Gascoigne, is he going to have a crack? He is!" All Spurs fans will remember that glorious moment at Wembley in 1991, as a 35-yard free-kick screamer from Gazza marked the beginning of a 3-1 demolition of arch rivals Arsenal in the FA Cup Semi-Final. It was typical of the silky skills and cheeky play that made Gazza a firm favourite at White Hart Lane. He left for Lazio shortly afterwards, but when he returns with Middlesbrough, he's assured a warm welcome.

SOL CAMPBELL

The Sol boy has been Tottenham's most consistent and promising player over the last few seasons. As the club have struggled through a lean period, he has been head and shoulders above the rest of the team – and not just because he's so tall! He has also blossomed into a handy international star and must rate as one of Europe's most skilfull defenders. Don't rule out a future England captaincy for him and Spurs fans will pray they can keep hold of him.

DID YOU KNOW?

Defender Justin Edinburgh is an Arsenal fan and one of his relatives' middle names is 'Merson'!

WHO'S THE GREATEST STRIKER?

Michael Owen showed just what he was made of during the World Cup Finals in France. But how does the Liverpool & England wonder boy measure up against the likes of Shearer, Bergkamp and Cole? SHOOT reveals all.

MICHAEL OWEN LIVERPOOL

AGE: 19

LOWDOWN: He doesn't muck about, does he? After just one full season of first-team football, Michael Owen forced his way into Glenn Hoddle's plans for the World Cup and even though he got limited chances to prove himself in France, managed to build himself a world wide reputation. No wonder European giants such as Juventus and Real Madrid were rumoured to be preparing £25million bids to secure his talents for themselves!

STRENGTHS: Pace and confidence. There isn't a defender in the world who wouldn't be terrified of coming up against someone has lightning quick as young Michael. He is also a cool customer who isn't fazed by pressure or nerves.

WEAKNESSES: He's never going to be a major aerial threat and he is sometimes easily provoked.

SHOOT RATING: 97

ALAN SHEARER NEWCASTLE

AGE: 29

LOWDOWN: He may have been plagued by injury worries and had only a moderately successful World Cup, but Super Al remains a major threat to any defence. His exploits down the years for the national side need no introduction and he's pretty handy in the league as well.

STRENGTHS: He is as solid as they come and defenders find it virtually impossible to shrug him off the ball. His other main strength? Oh, he's rather good at getting the ball into the back of the net!

WEAKNESSES: Has suffered from a series of serious injuries, and his temperament is coming under the microscope more and more as his career goes on.

SHOOT RATING: 95

✪ Each 'keeper is rated out of 100.

DENNIS BERGKAMP ARSENAL

AGE: 29
LOWDOWN: It was a close call, but the Dutch master Bergkamp just failed to sneak past his British rivals to the top of our striker's hit list. Following a mixed first season in English football, Bergy has become one of the best players, let alone strikers, in the country. He was on fire last season for 'The Gunners' and continued that form into the World Cup.
STRENGTHS: The word skill was created with players like Bergkamp in mind. His goals are always special, and he creates just as many chances for his team-mates. Quite simply, when Bergkamp's around, no defender or 'keeper can afford to relax for a moment.
WEAKNESSES: His temperament is suspect and he tends to take the law into his own hands if he feels he is being unfairly treated by opposing defenders. He also suffers badly when man-marked.
SHOOT RATING: 94

BRIAN LAUDRUP CHELSEA

AGE: 29
LOWDOWN: After starring in the Scottish Premiership for Rangers, Laudrup was a shrewd purchase by Blues boss Gianluca Vialli. He offers Chelsea a similar style of play to that which Dennis Bergkamp provides for Arsenal. He's quick, skillful and likes to make runs into the box from deep.
STRENGTHS: His adaptability means he can play up front, just off the main striker or drop back into midfield. Wherever Laudrup is on the field, he causes major problems for any defence because of his flash skills and pacey runs.
WEAKNESSES: He is not the strongest of players around and as such tends to attract heavy tactics from opposing defenders desperate to put him off his game.
SHOOT RATING: 92

JOHN HARTSON WEST HAM

AGE: 23
LOWDOWN: After starring at Arsenal and scoring in a European Final, Hartson was as gobsmacked as the rest of us when Arsene Wenger let him go to West Ham. But he quickly became a crowd favourite at Upton Park, first saving the club from relegation, then taking them to the brink of European qualification.
STRENGTHS: Power, power, power. Whether it's in the air or on the ground, Hartson is the most powerful striker around and can shrug off even the strongest defenders.
WEAKNESSES: Still prone to fits of temper and on-going vendettas against opponents, Hartson needs to cool it.
SHOOT RATING: 90

ANDY COLE MAN UNITED

AGE: 27
LOWDOWN: It's been an up-and-down career for Cole so far. After being sold by Arsenal, he eventually found his way to St James' Park where he was lethal in front of goal. When Alex Ferguson snapped him up, many expected Cole to make Man United invincible but his mixed form has disappointed many. He's now back on his game and set to cause havoc in the box once again.
STRENGTHS: His time at Old Trafford has improved Cole's all round game and he is now just as effective at holding up the ball and creating space, as he is finding the net itself. On his day, he is simply unstoppable.
WEAKNESSES: Very much a confidence player, Coley is prone to long periods of ineffectiveness when his head is down.
SHOOT RATING: 88

DWIGHT YORKE ASTON VILLA

AGE: 27
LOWDOWN: One of the Premiership's most consistently effective players, Yorkie has thrilled the Villa Park faithful with his flash tricks and lethal shooting in front of goal. He's also one of the most cheerful sights in the game, as he can't stop smiling!
STRENGTHS: A balanced player, he can dance his way around defenders to get into dangerous positions in front of goal. He's also pacey and sharp, so he's pretty much everything defenders dread!
WEAKNESSES: Not always effective in the air and he's played with so many different strike partners over the years he has never had the chance to settle into a balanced partnership.
SHOOT RATING: 87

KEVIN DAVIES BLACKBURN

AGE: 21
LOWDOWN: One moment he was plying his trade for lowly Chesterfield, the next he's starring for mighty Blackburn in the top-flight, following a brief stop at Southampton. It has been quite a fairy story for Davies and he is definitely one for England's future. Let's hope he gels well with Michael Owen, when the time comes!
STRENGTHS: His well-built physique makes him hard to shrug off the ball and he just seems to have that predatory striker's instinct in front of goal. Good from set-pieces as well.
WEAKNESSES: Having come so far in such a short space of time, it is important that he keeps himself in check and doesn't let the pressure – or the hype – bother him.
SHOOT RATING: 86

EMILE HESKEY LEICESTER

AGE: 20
LOWDOWN: One of the most powerful strikers around, Emile Heskey is loved at Filbert Street for his lethalness in front of goal. Sure to become a multi-million pound transfer subject before long, he should also be in with a shout of full international honours with England.
STRENGTHS: His main strength is his strength! Would you want to try and shrug Emile off the ball? He is also a major threat from set-pieces and is one of those awkward strikers that defenders dread facing in the air.
WEAKNESSES: Not the paciest player around, he needs to work on that side of his game to become the complete package.
SHOOT RATING: 85

LES FERDINAND TOTTENHAM

AGE: 32
LOWDOWN: The former QPR favourite returned to London to join Spurs after a successful period at Newcastle. Despite suffering from the inevitable White Hart Lane injury problems, he continues to star and was part of the England France '98 squad.
STRENGTHS: Aerial power. David Ginola, who has seen a few talents in his time, still rates Les as the best header of the ball he has seen.
WEAKNESSES: Injuries have meant he has been unable to make a real impression on the game for a while and he tends to let his head drop when the going gets tough – which it has been at Spurs for a while.
SHOOT RATING: 84

DARREN HUCKERBY COVENTRY

22
LOWDOWN: One of the revelations of last season, Huckerby scored a series of crucial goals for Gordon Strachan's men, including wonder strikes against Liverpool and Man United. Definitely in with a shout for England honours after his appearances for the 'B' side.
STRENGTHS: Pace and tricks. When Huckerby's running on or off the ball, he causes havoc for opposing defenders. It's hard to keep up with him and he turns very effectively at lightning quick pace.
WEAKNESSES: Not the biggest threat in the air and occasionally loses confidence when one-on-one on goal.
SHOOT RATING: 82

ALL THE TOP INFO ON ALL YOUR FAVE STARS!

NO.4

KEVIN GALLACHER

ON THE TEAM HE DREAMED OF PLAYING FOR WHEN HE WAS A KID

"It was Celtic. In fact when I was a kid, Billy McNeill was manager at the time and I went to see him about joining them. A couple of things changed my mind, though. Billy thought I was a bit frail and should go on the Guinness to build myself up! I was only 13 at the time!"

ON HIS FIRST CHILDHOOD IDOL

"Without a doubt it was the man Kenny Dalglish. I watched him when he was at Celtic and always followed his career when he joined Liverpool. He was an exceptional talent and it was great to get to work with him when he was manager of Blackburn."

ON LEAVING SCOTLAND

"It was a wrench. I enjoyed my time at Dundee United and I still support Celtic – it's been in my blood since I was a kid. The hardest thing was the language barrier – I had to talk very slowly for a while! I'm really enjoying it down here now though, because football has really taken off in England. I've no regrets at all."

ON ALL THE INJURIES HE'S SUFFERED

"When I first broke my leg I was told I would be out for six months, but that ended up being 11. I then broke it again 12 weeks later, which wrote another season off. When you're out for that amount of time you do get forgotten about. Nobody wants to know you until you come back. After nearly having my career taken away from me it has taught me about what I could lose."

ON SUCCESS IN HIS THIRTIES

"It's brilliant the way things have gone for me, and I'm on cloud nine. Things are definitely as good as they've ever been in the game for me, and I'll enjoy every minute of it. I'm determined to make up for the year-and-a-half that I missed with broken legs."

ON THE UPTURN IN BLACKBURN'S FORTUNES

"Yeah, one minute we were fighting relegation and the next we were challenging for the title. I think we all just needed a good kick up the backside in the summer of '97, and Roy Hodgson came in and did just that. The way we have been playing under Roy, we deserved to be up there."

ON ROVERS BOSS ROY HODGSON

"He took us back to basics, really. He gets us focusing on the basic technical aspects of the game to improve our passing, and it works. We're passing the ball so well and it allows you to step up and improve. He also believes in quality, not quantity. It's short intense bursts."

ON ROVERS' CHAMPIONSHIP CHANCES THIS SEASON

"Our aim is simple – to win the League either this season or next. It would be so nice to be part of a Championship winning team rather than in the squad like last time. We're happy to sit in behind the leaders and surprise them come the end of the season. We prefer a low profile – when we won the league in 1995 no-one seriously expected us to win it then either."

ON HIS FORM FOR ROVERS LAST SEASON

"It was definitely my most consistent season, and that's down to playing nearly all year in one position. I played only about five games out wide, but I much prefer it playing centre forward. I find it hard out on the wing because you can go five or ten minutes without seeing the ball sometimes, and I like to be involved all the time. In the centre I can keep making my runs, tackling back and getting involved in the action much more."

adidas
Co-operative
asics
BRFC

LEAGUE CUP 1988

LUTON v ARSENAL

24TH APRIL 1988:
LUTON 3-2 ARSENAL (HT:1-0)

LUTON TOWN: Dibble, Breacker, Johnson, Hill, Foster, Donaghy, Wilson, Stein B, Harford (sub: M. Stein), Preece (sub: Grimes).
Scorers: B. Stein (2), Wilson
ARSENAL: Lukic, Winterburn, Sansom, Thomas, Caeser, Adams, Rocastle, Davis, Smith, Groves (sub: Hayes), Richardson.
Scorers: Hayes, Smith
REFEREE: J. Worrall (Warrington)
ATT: 95,732 (At Wembley)

STAR MAN BRIAN STEIN

Just under 100,000 people saw little Luton snatch victory from the jaws of defeat, as the team from Bedfordshire won their first major trophy. Arsenal were awarded a penalty in the 81st minute and the possibility of a 3-1 lead. However, 'The Hatters" 'keeper Andy Dibble managed a fabulous dive to his left to save Nigel Winterburn's spot-kick. Earlier Brian Stein's first-half strike was cancelled out by goals from Gunners duo Martin Hayes and Alan Smith.

Danny Wilson equalized for Luton with a stooping header just after Winterburn's penalty miss. With extra-time looming substitute Ashley Grimes went on a determined run down the right and whipped in a pin-point cross for Brian Stein to notch his second, so ensuring Arsenal would not retain the trophy they had won 12 months earlier. In Luton's post- match celebrations they accidentally broke the famous trophy!

MOMENT OF THE MATCH

With extra-time looming Luton sub Ashley Grimes crossed the ball with the outside of his left foot and Brian Stein swept in the winner with just 14 seconds left on the clock.

HOW THEY MADE THE FINAL

LUTON	ARSENAL
R2 1st leg v Wigan 1-0	R2 1st leg v Doncaster 3-0
R2 2nd leg v Wigan 4-2	R2 2nd leg v Doncaster 1-0
R3 v Coventry 3-1	R3 v Bournemouth 3-0
R4 v Ipswich 1-0	R4 v Stoke 3-0
SF 1st leg v Oxford 1-1	SF 1st leg v Everton 1-0
SF 2nd leg v Oxford 2-0	SF 2nd leg v Everton 3-1

EVERYTHING YOU WANTED TO KNOW ABOUT

Leeds United were one of the country's most successful sides in the 1960s and '70s winning every domestic trophy going! But then it all went wrong and they had to wait until 1992 for their next trophy when they won the first ever Premiership title. Now ex-Arsenal boss George Graham wants to recreate the old glory days at Elland Road with a new Leeds side. So if you want to know about the past and present at Yorkshire's biggest club, read on for the Leed-ing guide to United!

FORMED: 1919
GROUND: Elland Road
NICKNAME: 'United'
RECORD LEAGUE VICTORY: 8-0 v Leicester City April 7th, 1934.
MOST LEAGUE APPEARANCES: Jack Charlton – 629 appearances (1953-73).
MOST CAPPED PLAYER: Billy Bremner – 54 caps for Scotland.
PLAYER WITH MOST LEAGUE GOALS: Peter Lorimer – 168 (1965-79 & 1983-86).
TOP SCORER 1997/98 (LEAGUE): Jimmy Floyd Hasselbaink 16

HONOURS: LEAGUE CHAMPIONS: 1968-69; 1973-74; 1991-92. **FA CUP:** 1972. **LEAGUE CUP:** 1968. **UEFA CUP:** 1968; 1971.

THE COUNTRY'S BIGGEST CLUBS!

GREAT MANAGER HOWARD WILKINSON

He took Leeds United into the top-flight and they finished an impressive fourth in their first season in 1991. Just a year later they were crowned Premiership Champions ahead of Manchester United. He is now Technical Director of the Football Association.

WHAT A STAR LEEDS' GREAT PLAYERS

GORDON STRACHAN

The flame haired Scotsman was the midfield orchestrator at Elland Road and his pulsating performances were matched by his infectious enthusiasm. He won the Footballer Of The Year Award in 1991 and skippered Leeds to the Premiership title in 1992. Now manager of Coventry, he put his remarkable engine as a player down to eating loads of bananas. So if you want to be the next midfield ace, eat loads of 'em and pray your hair doesn't turn ginger!

NIGEL MARTYN

Nigel Martyn's electric reflexes, safe hands and postional sense make him a crowd favourite at Elland Road. He was Britain's first £1million Keeper when Crystal Palace signed him from Bristol Rovers in 1989 and playing for a huge side like Leeds has helped improve his game even further. That has led to his entry on the international scene, and he currently competes with Tim Flowers for the chance to suceed David Seaman in the England No.1 shirt.

JIMMY HASSELBAINK

Jimmy who? That was the question that was on everyone's lips when George Graham brought the Dutchman to Elland Road in 1997. But after hitting the ground running, the six foot striker hit 16 goals in 35 games. His trademark 'semi-somersault' celebration has brightened up many a Premiership ground this season and opposing defences are now asking an entirely different new question of him – 'Why does he keep getting past us!?'

DID YOU KNOW?

Leeds wing-back Gary Kelly is the uncle of United defender Ian Harte.

A-Z OF SCOTTISH FOOTBALL

A is for ARBROATH

The wee Scottish side, formed in 1878, still holds perhaps the most enduring senior football record of them all – a 36-0 victory. The amazing result came in a cup-tie in 1885 against Aberdeen-based side Bon Accord. That's a goal every two-and-a-half minutes! The other less distinguished accolade they hold is that in 120 years of football they still haven't won anything, but have finished Second Division runners-up four times.

B is for BERWICK RANGERS

Rangers are notable in Scottish football as being the only English club that takes part in Scottish competitions. Since joining the league in 1951 their main concern has been survival, apart from one exceptional result conjured in 1967 when they beat the mighty Glasgow Rangers 1-0 in a cup match at their Shielfield Park ground. Celtic fans naturally gleaned particular pleasure upon hearing the result and many Bhoys supporters can tell you exactly where they were when they heard their fierce rivals had lost to the minnows.

C is for CURSE OF SCOTLAND

Scotland proved two things once again this summer. Not only are they seemingly incapable of qualifying for the second phase of the World Cup, but they also have an incredible knack of 'cursing' any rival teams in their group. Not one team in the history of the World Cup has ever become world champs with Scotland in their group. The theory was proved yet again this year, with Brazil falling at the last hurdle. Ronaldo had a convulsive fit? Hmm, sounds like the curse to us. Rumour has it the curse will only be broken once Scotland qualifies for the second phase at the ninth attempt!

D is for DENIS LAW

These days he earns a crust as a TV pundit but Denis Law also happens to be the only Scottish player to ever win the European Footballer Of The Year award. He's also known for his exploits as one of Matt Busby's revered Man United team of the late 1960s, where he was known as 'The King'. Legend has it that he was seriously upset after scoring a famous backheeled goal against United for their arch rivals Man City in 1974. The goal helped his former club get relegated to the Second Division! Arsenal and Holland superstar Dennis Bergkamp is also named after him!

E is for ESTONIA

In a World Cup qualifying fixture in 1997, Scotland couldn't believe their luck when they kicked off to find that Estonia had not bothered to turn up for their own home fixture. Initial reports were that Scotland would be awarded a 5-0 victory, but celebrations were premature as they were not given the three points after all. In fact, Craig Brown's men were ordered to replay the fixture in a neutral country. Scotland were ultimately frustrated in their attempts to score and were held to a 0-0 draw by the Eastern European minnows. Doh!

F is for FIXTURE CONGESTION

Football falls foul of this problem year upon year, but not quite as bad as the logjam Celtic found themselves in during the 1915-16 season. 'The Bhoys' had the unenviable task of playing two games in one day. They duly obliged beating Raith Rovers 6-0, followed by an away match at Motherwell, which they won 3-1. In 1981 Queen Of The South found themselves in a bizarre situation as two different teams arrived to play on the same afternoon. Fortunately for the 'Doonhammers' one of those sides had made a mistake after all!

G is for GOALKEEPERS

Scotland has an uneviable reputation in providing the world with some of the best examples of 'calamity 'keeping'. A case in point has to be the unfortunate Frank Haffey, who had what some managers might describe as a 'shocker' when he was on the wrong end of a 9-3 thrashing. To make matters worse the opponents were the 'Auld enemy' England, with the young Jimmy Greaves bagging a hat-trick in the 1961 rout. Scotland fans were endlessly taunted by the result (legend has it that a record of the match commentary was released!) Fortunately for the Scots, revenge arrived with a 2-1 win in 1963 and more significantly in 1967 (see W is for Wembley Wizards).

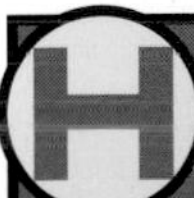

H is for HAMPDEN PARK

The current Hampden Park is the third stadium of that name to have existed in Scotland and was built in 1903. Until 1950 it was the largest footie ground in the world and in 1937 set an attendance record for a match between two club sides when 145,000 punters crammed in to watch Celtic take on Aberdeen. The stadium topped that in the same year when 150,000 fans turned up to see Scotland take on England.

I is for IBROX DISASTER

Tragedy struck not once, but twice this century at Rangers' famous Ibrox Park stadium. First in 1902, thought to be the world's first major football disaster, 26 people were killed and 500 injured during the Scotland v England home international when a newly extended wooden stand collapsed and fans fell through a hope in the structure. The second Ibrox disaster occurred in 1971, when during a Ranger v Celtic match 66 fans lost their lives and 140 were injured in a massive crush on the notorious Stairway 13 in the Rangers end. The resulting enquiry resulted in the Safety Of Sports Grounds Act being introduced in 1975. At the time this was the worst football tragedy that Britain had witnessed.

J is for JAM TARTS

The nickname of Scottish Premiership side Hearts (it rhymes, you see!). The side are properly known as Heart Of Midlothian, taking their name from an old prison in their home city of Edinburgh. Described by their fans as 'the nearly men of Scottish football', 'The Jam Tarts' yet again lived up to that tag last season by finishing third in the Scottish Premier League, despite being joint top for most of the campaign. However, Hearts sought consolation in the FA Cup Final, beating Rangers 2-1, much to their long-suffering fans' delight. The Edinburgh club are one of the few Scottish teams capable of challenging the Celtic/Rangers status quo, but lack the resources to attract big name players. However, their young, mostly Scottish team has won them lots of fans amongst neutrals.

K is for KING KENNY

The nickname given to the man who someone once described as having 'as much personality as a tennis racket' – Kenny Dalglish. He started his glittering career at Celtic in 1970, helping them win seven trophies as a stylish attacking player. Dalglish went on to win 102 caps with Scotland and countless medals with Liverpool before becoming a player-manager with the Merseyside club. He went on to win three league titles at Anfield before suddenly 'retiring' in 1991, although he reappeared eight months later at Blackburn where he won the English Premiership title in 1995. King Kenny is currently Newcastle boss, where the going has been tough for perhaps the first time in his career, despite strong financial backing.

L is for LISBON LIONS

The name given to Jock Stein's all-conquering Celtic team who triumphed 2-1 against Inter Milan in 1967 to become the first British team to win the European Cup. Club folklore says that some of the supporters were so overcome by that night in Portugal that they settled there permanently. Celtic made it to the Final once again three years later, but were defeated 2-1 by Feyenoord, beginning a Dutch domination of the competition. No Scottish team has since made it to the Final of Europe's premier cup comp and it is now 11 years since Dundee United became the last team to represent the country in a European Final.

A-Z OF SCOTTISH FOOTBALL

 is for MANAGERS

Despite Scotland's international standing declining in recent decades, Scotland has continued its proud boast of providing football with some of the canniest managers in the game. The managerial legacy of Jock Stein (Celtic), Matt Busby (Man United) and Bill Shankly (Liverpool) has continued with Alex Feguson, George Graham and Kenny Dalglish collecting the lions share of the English silverware on offer over the past decade. Also worthy of a mention is Craig Brown and Andy Roxburgh's achievements of qualifying Scotland for several major international tournaments despite a desperate lack of genuine world class talent.

 is for NINE IN A ROW

Both Celtic (1966-74) and more recently Rangers (1989-1997) have managed the superlative feat of winning the Scottish League title nine times on the spin. In fact, Rangers were only denied a record breaking tenth title in a row when Celtic beat them to the Scottish Championship by two points last season. The blue half of Glasgow shouldn't be too upset though, their side has won an amazing 46 titles to Celtic's 35. 'The Bhoys' will need another 11 on the trot to equal it!

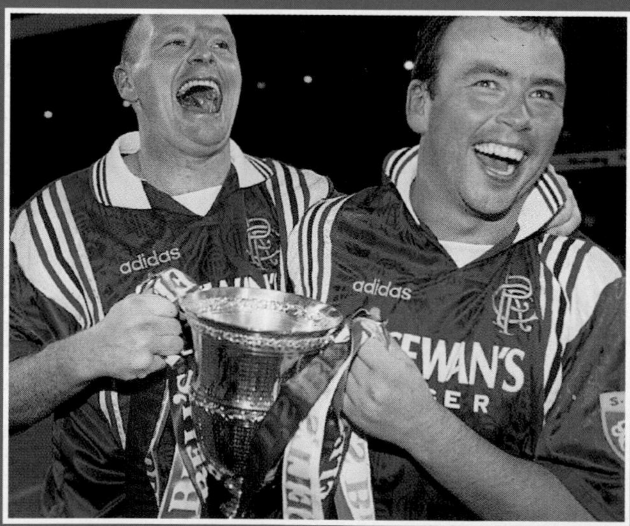

 is for OLD FIRM DERBY

Rangers v Celtic – possibly the fiercest local rivalry anywhere in world football and unquestionably the biggest fixture in the Scottish domestic calendar. Played four times a season (not counting potential cup encounters) between the bitter Glasgow rivals, the hostilities stretch considerably further than football, with religious, cultural and historical differences to take into account.

 is for PREMIER LEAGUE

English football may have only had its own Premier League since 1992 but in Scotland they've had one since 1975! The first winners of the title were Rangers (surprise, surprise!) and since it was launched only two teams – Aberdeen (1980, 1984, 1985) and Dundee United (1983) – have won it apart from the two big Glasgow clubs.

 is for QUEEN'S PARK

Otherwise known as 'The Spiders'. One of the most peculiar contradictions in world football is that one of the oldest (founded 1867) and worst supported clubs in Scottish football are the occupants of the glorious Hampden Park – the home of Scottish football. The team regularly turn out to one man and his dog, although they pride themselves on maintaining their amateur status 131 years on. The English league equivalent would be Brentford playing at Wembley. Queen's Park also claim to be the first team to adopt the three o'clock kick off.

 is for RESIGNATION

Because of a lack of progress in Europe by Scottish clubs in the last decade it has been suggested that the Scottish Premier League isn't of a high enough standard for the likes of Celtic and Rangers, and that to improve they both need regular top quality opposition. Some pundits and fans even think the sides should quit Scotland and join the English Premiership where they'd face the mighty Charlton and Wimbledon. Hmm...

 is for SCOTTISH CUP

One of the oldest cup competitions in the world, set up in 1873. Fifteen clubs contributed to the purchase of the first trophy, at a total cost of £56, 12shillings and 11pence (that's old money and it were a lot in them days!) Current standings for the most successful teams in the cup are, you guessed it, Celtic, closely followed by Rangers. Aberdeen deserve a mention as well, for winning the cup four times in the glory days of the '80s under Alex Ferguson's management. Minnows East Fife managed to win the Cup in 1938 and became the only side to achieve the feat while a lowly Second Division side. For the most famous Scottish FA Cup match see A is for Arbroath.

T is for TARTAN ARMY

Affectionate nickname given to Scotland's hoard of incredibly loyal travelling fans who accompany their beloved team wherever they go. At France '98 the Scottish supporters were so well regarded they were awarded the title of the tournament's best fans. Such excellent behaviour has gone a long way to repairing their image of the 1970s, when Scottish fans were perceived as hard drinking and violent. The hard man image has gone but the hard drinking remains the same!

U is for UEFA RANKING

Year upon year of European disappointments has ensured that Scottish clubs have been, in recent seasons, denied an automatic place in the prestigious Champions League by UEFA – having to battle through tricky qualifiers in obscure eastern European countries instead! Despite winning nine Scottish League titles in a row Rangers have again and again failed to translate that kind of form on to the European stage. They were dumped out of the European Cup in 1994 by the not so mighty Levski Sofia and having made it to the Champions League stage in 1996 went on to win just one of their group games, losing once to Grasshoppers Of Zurich and twice to both Auxerre and Ajax. The Glasgow club's last decent run in the competition came in 1992 when they made the final eight.

V is for VALE OF LEVEN

A member of the Scottish League from 1890 to 1926, they were once considered to be the strongest team in Scottish football. They are thought to be still active in Scotland, playing in the minor leagues.

W is for WEMBLEY WIZARDS

Depending on your age this title went to two different Scottish international teams. The original (and possibly best) was the 1928 side which thrashed the supposedly invincible England 5-1, a result still cherished north of the border. The line up included the likes of Alex James (not the Blur bassist!) and Hughie Gallacher. The second legendary team scored a sweet 3-2 victory in April 1967 and became the first side to beat the recently crowned World Champions. The result helped to wipe away the humiliating memory of the 9-3 drubbing dished out by England six years previously.

X is for MISTER X

The name given to a mystery Morton goalkeeper during a practice match in 1964, something which led to fevered speculation about his identity. It was eventually revealed to the public that the 'keeper was Danish international Eric Sorensen, who, incidentally, also became the first Scandinavian player to make an impact on the Scottish game.

Y is for YOUNG, GEORGE

Captained Scotland a record 48 times during the 1950s, also set a record of 34 consecutive appearances in the blue and white jersey (later bettered by Kenny Dalglish). A formidable defender, regarded as the best of his era. Despite captaining Scotland eight times against England, Young never had the pleasure of beating them at Hampden Park, but was a winner at Wembley in 1949 and '51.

Z is for ZZZzzz

Some players, notably former Celtic striker Pierre Van Hooijdonk, found playing each rival team in the Scottish Premier League four times every season a real drag. The idea is to maximise crowds for big games such as Celtic v Rangers and Hearts v Hibernian. It's a bit boring though, isn't it?!

ALL THE TOP INFO ON ALL YOUR FAVE STARS!

NO.5

JOHN HARTSON

WEST HAM

ON HIS ABILITY AS A TOP GOALSCORER

"I have faith in my own ability as a striker and I know that if I'm given a decent run in a side that I can always score goals. Obviously, I enjoy it when the goals are coming, but I know just how quickly the goals can dry up. I just hope I can continue scoring for West Ham."

ON SETTING GOALSCORING TARGETS BEFORE THE START OF THE SEASON

"The most important thing is not my goalscoring, but the team's performance. West Ham's aim must be to build on last season's success by finishing in a European place and having a couple of good cup runs. I've played in a European Final with Arsenal and I'd love to do the same with West Ham.

ON LEARNING FROM IAN WRIGHT AND DENNIS BERGKAMP AT ARSENAL

"Both of them are great players and you couldn't help but admire their talents in training. Wright is a great guy and Dennis is the model pro on and off the field.

It's just nice now to be regarded as a first choice striker every week."

ON BRITAIN'S TOP STRIKER

"Alan Shearer is obviously the pinnacle for everybody to try and match in this country. When you look at his goal scoring record at club and international level, it really is quite phenomenal. Without a doubt he's one of the best strikers in the world and I'm sure he'd have bagged a lot more goals in the World Cup had England got past Argentina."

ON BATTLING FOR A PLACE AT HIGHBURY

"I think I would still struggle to get a place, to be fair, unless Wenger decided to play with three strikers! I think with the way their front players performed last season, it would still have been very difficult for me to get a game."

ON IMPROVEMENTS IN HIS GAME SINCE LEAVING HIGHBURY FOR WEST HAM

"I think I have made improvements in the way that I play since the move, but I'm only young and still need to work on certain aspects of my game. The added responsibility of being the No.1 striker has helped me, because I seem to be able to express myself more. Playing every week helps any player improve their game and hopefully that will continue in my case."

ON HIS FOOTIE HERO AS A KID

"Ian Rush was my all-time hero, so naturally I was a Liverpool fan when I was a youngster. I never got the chance to see them play as I lived in south Wales. Swansea were my local team abck then, so my dad usually took me along to see them. I had plenty of Liverpool posters on my walls though! I don't follow them now – I prefer to keep a look out for the teams I have played for in the past, like Luton and Arsenal."

SCOTTISH FA CUP 1996
RANGERS v HEARTS

MAY 18th 1996
RANGERS 5-1 HEARTS (HT: 1-0)

RANGERS: Goram, Cleland, Robertson, Gough, McLaren, Brown, Durie, Gascoigne, Ferguson (sub: Durrant), McCall, Laudrup. Scorers: Laudrup (2), Durie (3)
HEARTS: Roussett; Locke (sub: Lawrence), Ritchie, McManus, McPherson, Bruno (sub: Robertson), Johnston, Mackay, Colquhoun, Fulton, Pointon. Scorer: Colquhoun
REFEREE: H. Dallas (Motherwell)
ATT: 37,730 (At Hampden Park)

STAR MAN GORDON DURIE

Brian Laudrup put on a sizzling performance at Hampden Park as 'Gers won their third double in five years by overwhelming the men from Edinburgh. Hearts suffered the misfortune of losing skipper Gary Locke with a twisted knee in the sixth minute of the match and it was all downhill from there. Laudrup gave Rangers a first half lead and he soon doubled it in the 52 minute after his cross/shot squirmed through the legs of Gilles Roussett in the Hearts goal.

Durie then became the first player for 24 years to score a hat-trick in a Scottish Cup Final when all his goals were laid on a plate by the dazzling display from rampant Danish international Laudrup. Hearts managed a consolation goal from veteran John Colquhoun but it was not enough to prevent Rangers claiming their 27th Scottish Cup triumph.

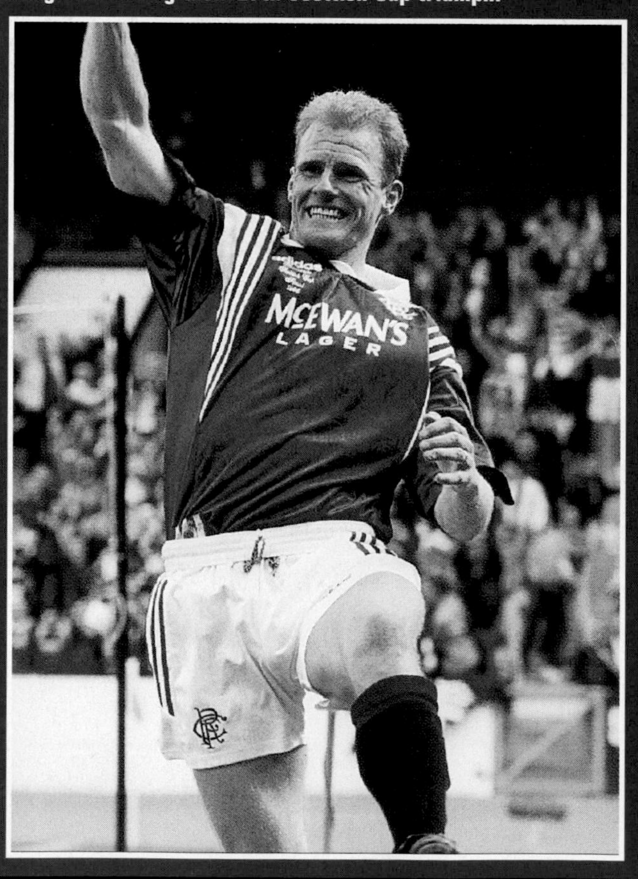

MOMENT OF THE MATCH

Early in the second half, dynamic Dane Brian Laudrup hit a cross/shot which beat Hearts 'keeper Roussett at his near post and it was all one-way traffic after that.

HOW THEY MADE THE FINAL

RANGERS	HEARTS
R3 v Keith 10-1	R3 v Partick 1-0
R4 v Clyde 4-1	R4 v Kilmarnock 2-1
QF v Caledonian Thistle 3-1	QF v St Johnstone 2-1
SF v Celtic 2-1	SF v Aberdeen 2-1

EVERYTHING YOU WANTED TO KNOW ABOUT EVERTON

It may have been a sticky time for 'The Toffeemen' last season, but Everton are still a massive name in British football. Winning nine league titles and five FA Cups, the Merseyside giants have a proud history and tradition. Now the pressure of that tradition rests on the shoulders of Big Duncan Ferguson, young Danny Cadamarteri and Everton's new breed of heroes. So, for the sweetest guide to 'The Toffeemen' you'll ever find, read on as SHOOT dips into the Goodison Park history book!

FORMED: 1878
GROUND: Goodison Park
NICKNAME: 'The Toffees'
RECORD LEAGUE VICTORY: 9-1 v Manchester City September 3rd 1906.
MOST LEAGUE APPEARANCES: Neville Southall – 570 (1981-97).
MOST CAPPED PLAYER: Neville Southall – 91 caps for Wales.
PLAYER WITH MOST LEAGUE GOALS: Dixie Dean – 349 (1925-37).
TOP SCORER 1997/98 (LEAGUE): Duncan Ferguson 11

HONOURS: LEAGUE CHAMPIONS: 1890-91; 1914-15; 1927-28; 1931-32; 1938-39; 1962-63; 1969-70; 1984-85; 1986-87.
FA CUP: 1906; 1933; 1966; 1984; 1995. **EUROPEAN CUP WINNERS CUP:** 1985.

THE COUNTRY'S BIGGEST CLUBS!

GREAT MANAGER HOWARD KENDALL

Amazingly, Howard has had three spells as Everton boss. But his association with the Goodison side goes back even further – he played for them in the 1964 FA Cup Final! In his time Howard has led Everton to two league titles, one FA Cup and one European Cup Winners Cup.

WHAT A STAR EVERTON'S GREAT PLAYERS

GARY LINEKER

The 'Football Focus' presenter spent one season at Everton in the mid-'80s. He scored 30 league goals as well as one in the 1986 FA Cup Final. Unfortunately, Everton finished runners-up to Liverpool in both the Championship and FA Cup.

However, Lineker won both Player Of The Year awards and won the Golden Boot at the Mexico World Cup in 1986. Spanish giants Barcelona prised him away from Goodison for £2.75million after the finals had finished.

NEVILLE SOUTHALL

The Welsh veteran made his debut for Everton in 1981 and helped them to two league titles, an FA Cup and European Cup Winners' Cup in his time at Goodison Park. Big Nev became a legend on Merseyside and it was strange to watch 'The Toffeemen' play without him last season after he was replaced by Norwegian shot-stopper, Thomas Myre. As a result Nev ended up on loan to Southend and Stoke City, but his future surely belongs in management.

DUNCAN FERGUSON

Big Dunc is the heart and soul of everything that happens at Goodison Park. A born leader, he is one of the world's most competitive players and is never scared to put his foot in where it hurts. His aerial presence is well documented, but his ability, skill and pace with the ball at his feet is cruelly underated. His international career with Scotland might have come to a premature end but his heroics for Everton continue. A real star.

DID YOU KNOW?

Everton's Goodison Park is nicknamed 'Toffeeopolis'. Strange, eh?

WHO'S THE GREATEST GOALKEEPER?

The Premiership might not necessarily have the best defenders, midfielders or attackers in the world but when it comes to 'keepers the English top-flight is second to none! But which top stopper is the best? SHOOT reveals all.

DAVID SEAMAN ARSENAL

AGE: 35

LOWDOWN: One of SHOOT's greatest mates in the game, Seamo is much more than a man with a dodgy moustache. A national hero after his exploits for England, he is also a firm favourite with the Highbury faithful. He's helped Arsenal win two league titles, two FA Cups, the League Cup and the European Cup Winners' Cup. And who can forget Euro '96? Good work fella!

STRENGTHS: We could go on all day! Seamo is an all round star, as cool on crosses as he is sweet with shot-stopping. But if he has an obvious strength above his rivals, it is he's absolute magic at penalties. For club and country, he has seen off more penalty shoot-outs than any other 'keeper around.

WEAKNESSES: Are you having a laugh? The word weakness doesn't even come into any discussion of Seamo! But if you insist, we would have to say: 'Nayim, from the halfway line!' Sorry, Dave!

SHOOT RATING: 99

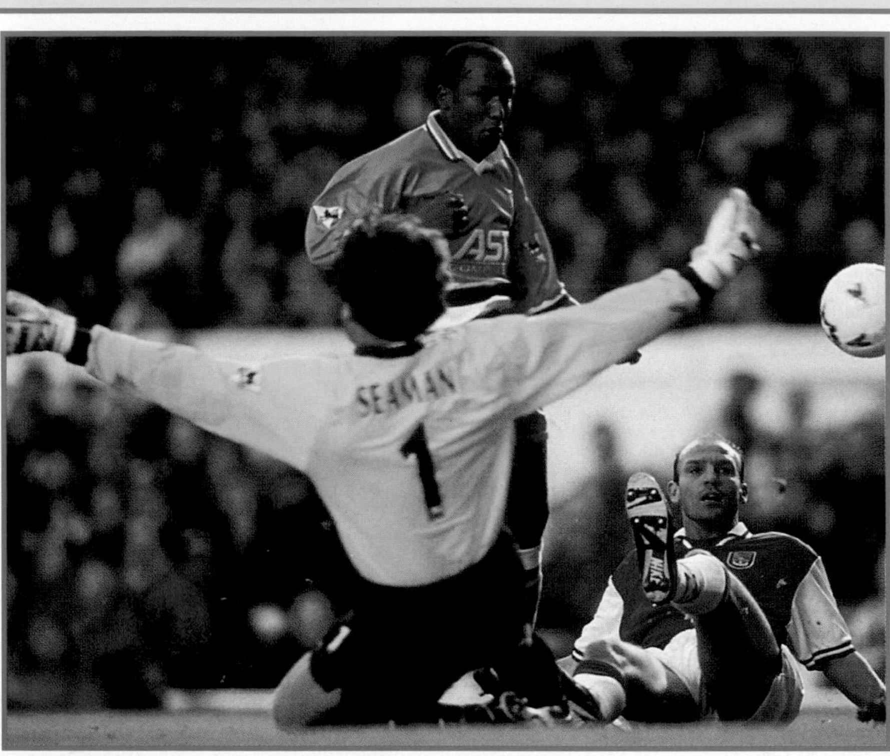

PETER SCHMEICHEL MAN UNITED

AGE: 35

LOWDOWN: It's a little known fact that Peter Schmeichel was once turned down by Newcastle, years before he joined Man United. But 'The Great Dane' had the last laugh when he helped 'The Reds' steal in to nick top spot from Newcastle and grab the 1996 title. One of the stroppiest players around, he would probably ring up Gary Neville and shout at him if he ran out of milk.

STRENGTHS: As Sky TV's Andy Gray says: 'How many times have we talked about this man making himself big and cutting out shots?' The answer, Andy, is far too many times, but that's not Schmeichel's fault! It's his main strength and his sheer presence seems to scare even the very best strikers into making mistakes.

WEAKNESSES: We've all heard the jokes about Schmeichel not liking chips and he certainly seems to have suffered plenty of red face moments when lobbed by cheeky strikers.

SHOOT RATING: 97

Each 'keeper is rated out of 100.

NIGEL MARTYN LEEDS

AGE: 33
LOWDOWN: Nige quietly built himself a good reputation during his time at Selhurst Park with Crystal Palace, before George Graham snapped him up to join his rebuilding job with Leeds at Elland Road. He has been involved with the national side as well and featured in England's pre-World Cup friendlies.
STRENGTHS: Shot-stopping is without doubt Nigel's main strength. As any Leeds fan will tell you, he is rarely beaten by shots from outside the area and he dominates his box well.
WEAKNESSES: Doubts continue to hover over whether Nigel communicates with his defenders enough. This most important part of any 'keeper's armoury seems to need a bit of extra work and attention from the Leeds No.1.
SHOOT RATING: 94

TIM FLOWERS BLACKBURN

AGE: 31
LOWDOWN: Its easy to forget that Tim has won a Premiership title with Blackburn and is only one of three goalkeepers who have that medal to their name. He has also been involved in the England set-up under three successive managers, Graham Taylor, Terry Venables and Glenn Hoddle. Highly rated in the game, he is a popular figure with his team-mates and fans.
STRENGTHS: Crosses. Flowers is one of the best 'keepers around for cutting out any balls whipped in from the flanks and he is very effective at corners as well. In the Premiership, where so many goals seem to come from such areas, that's a serious plus!
WEAKNESSES: Shots from a distance have often been the undoing of him. But then most 'keepers are caught out from time to time.
SHOOT RATING: 93

NEIL SULLIVAN WIMBLEDON

AGE: 28
LOWDOWN: Sully has come from nowhere to be one of the most respected 'keepers in the game, but one of the most under-rated by supporters. OK, so its easy to remember him as the victim of 'that' goal by David Beckham (and the one David Batty stuck by him a few days later!), but Dons supporters know he's extremely consistent!
STRENGTHS: Shot-stopping. He can cut out shots from inside the box or from miles out with ease, and is excellent on crosses as well. Sully also commands his penalty box well and has an excellent understanding with his defenders.
WEAKNESSES: The Beckham and Batty incidents aside (did he pay the Argentinians to get revenge for him?), Sully's main weakness is his near-post covering. The worst mistake a 'keeper can make is to be beaten at the near post, but Sully seems to manage it a bit too much!
SHOOT RATING: 91

ED DE GOEY CHELSEA

AGE: 30
LOWDOWN: When he first arrived from Holland, Ed de Goey was known for little more than looking like a deep sea monkfish on these shores. After a shaky start, he established himself as one of the Prem's top 'keepers and steered Chelsea to a double of the Coca-Cola Cup and European Cup Winners' Cup.
STRENGTHS: Big Ed is fantastic at cutting out volleys and he ain't bad at penalty shoot-outs either! He dominates his box well and now he is fully settled, his confidence seems to rise with every game.
WEAKNESSES: Occasionally, he tends to parry shots rather than hold onto them. These spillages can then lead to unneccesary goals.
SHOOT RATING: 89

ALEX MANNINGER ARSENAL

AGE: 20
LOWDOWN: When the floppy-haired Austrian arrived at Highbury, he probably expected to keep the bench warm rather than keep the goal safe. But thanks to an injury to first-choice David Seaman, Alex got his chance during possibly the most dramatic league run-in in the club's history.
STRENGTHS: During the time he spent in the first-team, Alex seemed to have it all. He came out on top at penalty shoot-outs, claimed crosses well and stopped pretty much everything thrown (or kicked or headed) at him!
WEAKNESSES: To keep things in perspective, he hasn't yet been tested over a full season and had nothing to lose during the time he was in the first-team. He also makes dangerous runs out of his area when the striker is clean through on goal.
SHOOT RATING: 88

DAVID JAMES LIVERPOOL

AGE: 28
LOWDOWN: When he arrived at Anfield from Watford, the hair was a bit longer and his confidence a bit higher, yet David has bounced back well after a series of high profile mistakes.
STRENGTHS: His main strength is his reflexes to sudden shots and his distribution knocks the spots off most other Premiership 'keepers as well. Although he has been the butt of many supporters' jokes, they should remember that you don't get years of first-team action as Anfield easily!
WEAKNESSES: He may be 'cross' when he reads this, but David James has made some calamitous mistakes from crosses! When he comes out to catch them, he doesn't seem to communicate with his defenders well and such errors seem to happen more in 'big' matches.
SHOOT RATING: 86

SHAY GIVEN BLACKBURN

AGE: 22
LOWDOWN: The Republic Of Ireland international may look too stocky to be a 'keeper, but didn't he prove us wrong last season? Putting in some fantastic performances, Shay is now one of the Premiership's flashest goalkeepers!
STRENGTHS: Shay is the most courageous 'keeper around and loves diving for balls where there is a risk of a boot in the mouth! OK, so he may be slightly mad, but every club would love to have such a brave lad in goal!
WEAKNESSES: Sometimes his enthusiasm gets the better of him and he must think more about when to go for balls and when to let his defence tidy up.
SHOOT RATING: 85

IAN WALKER TOTTENHAM

AGE: 27
LOWDOWN: Following his father Mike's footsteps into the beautiful game, Ian has been a consistent performer at Spurs throughout the club's recent highs and lows. He has also forced his way onto the fringes of the England team and, at 27. still has a bright future ahead of him.
STRENGTHS: Ian's reflexes are razor sharp and that can save any club numerous points each season. He is also fantastic on crosses, corners and set-pieces. His distribution is also good.
WEAKNESSES: Ian's confidence seems to have taken a series of knocks during the recent problems that have beset White Hart Lane. It can't have been easy for him conceding six or seven goals in one game each season, when those scorelines were by no means all his fault.
SHOOT RATING: 84

SHAKA HISLOP WEST HAM

AGE: 29
LOWDOWN: After an unhappy season at Newcastle that saw him dropped from the side, Shaka signed for West Ham hoping to restart his career. He is also hoping to build on last season's involvement in the England 'B' team.
STRENGTHS: Shaka seems to be able to jump higher than any other human being on earth, and as such is absolutely fantastic on crosses. He also seems to dominate his box well.
WEAKNESSES: We're all prone to lapses in concentration, but when you are a 'keeper and that happens, you will always be punished. Shaka seems to lose his head at just the wrong moment. Oops!
SHOOT RATING: 82

ALL THE TOP INFO ON ALL YOUR FAVE STARS!

NO.6 FRANK LEBOEUF

CHELSEA

ON LEAVING FRANCE FOR LONDON

"I wanted a new motivation. When I was at Strasbourg, I was just going through the motions. I was really bored – I felt like I was playing in the Third Division, in small grounds with no atmosphere."

ON PLAYING FOOTBALL IN THE ENGLISH PREMIERSHIP

"The English are fanatical in the best sense of the word. I love playing in front of 30,000 people every game. I love the crowd and the all the noise. This state of mind would never exist in France and the lack of atmosphere really weighs on you."

ON CHELSEA'S CHAMPIONSHIP CHANCES

"Yes, I think following on from last season's success in the cups, we have to make that a target. Chelsea now have a lot of top quality players who are also very intelligent. I am confident and ambitious and I believe we can win the Championship. But you never know what can happen because any number of things can go wrong over the period of a few months – injuries, for example, can play a big role. Any team that wants to win must make sure that they stay injury free if possible. We must also become more consistent at Chelsea."

ON HIS AMBITIONS FOR THE BLUES

"We are all very ambitious at the club and I'm sure everyone is dreaming of the Champions' League for next season. I would like to play in it before I retire. If we can get there and continue to build on our squad, I'm sure we can win it."

ON CHELSEA'S MAIN RIVALS FOR TROPHIES THIS SEASON

"The Premiership is a very competitive league with a number of good sides who will be challenging fiercely. Apart from us of course, there is obviously Man United. Arsenal are also very dangerous opponents – they have a very strong team with very good players. I expect Liverpool and Blackburn to be up there with us. I have a lot of respect for Roy Hodgson – he is a great boss and has some very good players."

ON FRENCH MANAGER AIME JACQUET'S ATTITUDE TO ENGLISH FOOTBALL

"People have tried to make out that you cannot get into the French national side if you play for an English club just because the manager has left David Ginola and Eric Cantona out of his plans over the last few years. However, Vieira and Petit of Arsenal weren't in the national side before they came to England – Vieira didn't even have a cap before coming to Arsenal. I also played for the national side in the World Cup so you can't say that you won't get in the French side if you play in England."

ON PLAYING IN EUROPE ON A THURSDAY

"It doesn't help you prepare for a Premiership game on a Saturday or even a Sunday, that's for sure. You don't have enough time to recover, but we know the rules. You have to expect it when you are a successful club and doing well in more than one competition. You can swap around some players in the league games, but you can't change everyone. We have to sleep a lot between the two games!"

HELSEA FC

EUROPEAN CUP-WINNERS' CUP 1994

ARSENAL v PARMA

MAY 4th 1994

ARSENAL 1-0 PARMA (HT: 1-0)

ARSENAL: Seaman, Dixon, Winterburn, Davis, Bould, Adams, Campbell, Morrow, Smith, Merson (sub: McGoldrick), Selley.
Scorer: Smith
PARMA: Bucci, Benarrivo, Di Chiara, Minotti, Apolloni, Sensini, Brolin, Pin (sub: Melli), Crippa, Zola, Asprilla.
REFEREE: Krondl (Czech Republic)
ATT: 33,765 (in Copenhagen)

STAR MAN STEVE MORROW

The Northern Ireland International played a key role in central midfield marking Gianfranco Zola and pulled off a very assured and disciplined performance.

Arsenal won their second European trophy when they beat the holders and favourites Parma in Copenhagen. The magnificent Gunners scored the only goal in the 20th minute when a miscued overhead clearance fell to the feet of Alan Smith whose left-footed volley smashed into the net off the inside of the near post. A new anthem was born among the incredible support from the terraces: 'one-nil to the Arsenal'.

The under-strength Gunners then contained the Italians who included players such as Gianfranco Zola and Faustino Asprilla in their forward line. Arsenal manager George Graham, who had won every domestic honour in England, had now conquered Europe and become one of the most successful manager's in Arsenal's history.

MOMENT OF THE MATCH

A flash of brilliance by veteran striker Alan Smith when his spectacular volley powered into the Parma net. It was a lead Arsenal never looked like surrendering.

HOW THEY MADE THE FINAL

ARSENAL	PARMA
R1 1st leg v Odense 2-1	R1 1st leg v Degerfors 2-1
R1 2nd leg v Odense 1-1	R1 2nd leg v Degerfors 2-0
R2 1st leg v Standard Liege 3-0	R2 1st leg v Maccabi Haifa 1-0
R2 2nd leg v Standard Liege 7-0	R2 2nd leg v Maccabi Haifa 0-1
QF 1st leg v Torino 0-0	Parma won 3-1 on penalties
QF 2nd leg v Torino 1-0	QF 1st leg v Ajax 0-0
SF 1st leg v Paris St Germain 1-1	QF 2nd leg v Ajax 2-0
SF 2nd leg v Paris St Germain 1-0	SF 1st leg v Benfica 1-2
	SF 2nd leg v Benfica 1-0

EVERYTHING YOU WANTED TO KNOW ABOUT

MAN UTD

It's a mark of the success Alex Ferguson has brought to Old Trafford that last season was considered a disappointment even though 'The Red Devils' finished runners-up in the league, reached the Champions League Quarter-Finals and graced the Premiership with their flash footie skills! But did you know that until their 1993 title triumph United had gone an amazing 26 years without winning the league? Now find out more about the Man United story in SHOOT's definitive guide to the club.

FORMED: 1878
GROUND: Old Trafford
NICKNAME: 'The Red Devils'
RECORD LEAGUE VICTORY: 9-0 v Ipswich Town March 4th, 1995.
MOST LEAGUE APPEARANCES: Bobby Charlton – 606 appearances (1956-73).
MOST CAPPED PLAYER: Bobby Charlton – 106 caps for England.
PLAYER WITH MOST LEAGUE GOALS: Bobby Charlton – 199 goals (1956-73).
TOP SCORER 1997/98 (LEAGUE): Andy Cole 14

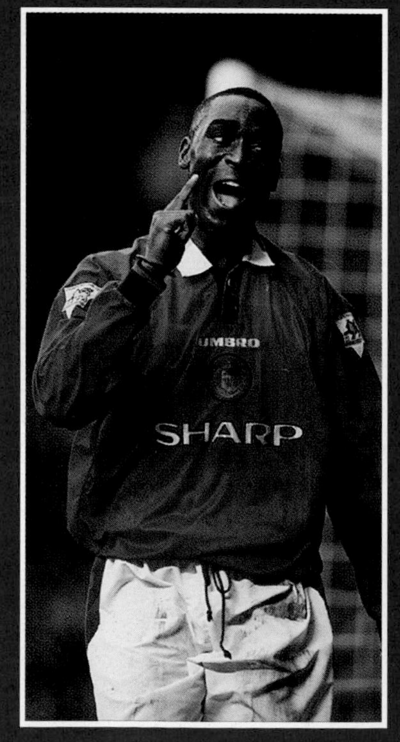

CHAMPIONS: 1907-08; 1910-11; 1951-52; 1955-56; 1956-57; 1964-65; 1966-67; 1992-93; 1993-94; 1995-96; 1996-97. **FA CUP:** 1909; 1948; 1963; 1977; 1983; 1985; 1990; 1994; 1996. **LEAGUE & FA CUP DOUBLE:** 1994; 1996. **LEAGUE CUP:** 1992. **EUROPEAN CUP:** 1968. **EUROPEAN CUP WINNERS CUP:** 1991. **EUROPEAN SUPER CUP WINNERS:** 1991.

THE COUNTRY'S BIGGEST CLUBS!

GREAT MANAGER ALEX FERGUSON

Currently the most successful boss in Football. Since moving south from Aberdeen he has collected four League titles, three FA Cups, a League Cup and the club's first European trophy in 23 years. Not the most popular man outside Old Trafford, he's loved by the United faithful.

WHAT A STAR MAN UTD'S GREAT PLAYERS

BRYAN ROBSON

'Captain Marvel' Bryan Robson was one of the most talented midfield players of the 1980s. He became the first captain to lift the FA Cup three times and skippered United to European and League Cup glory. Robson won 89 caps for England and scored the fastest goal in English international history when he bagged a goal against France just 27 seconds into the game at the 1982 World Cup Finals. Robbo is currently manager of Middlesbrough.

ERIC CANTONA

The Frenchman was signed from Leeds in 1992 and helped 'The Red Devils' to their first Championship in 26 years. He then inspired United to the Double with a brace in the 1994 FA Cup Final against Chelsea. Although controversy seemed to follow him wherever he went, Eric was adored at Old Trafford for his matchwinning skills. He retired from football at the age of 30 after winning his fifth Championship in six years and Alex Ferguson will be lucky to find as skillful a player again.

DAVID BECKHAM

Forget about his good looks and Spice Girl partner, it is on the pitch that David Beckham's talent really shows. Has there ever been an English midfielder with a better eye for goal than this young man? If there is, we'd love to hear about him! And how flash are his goals? Flash as you like! Already virtually guaranteed a place in the England team for the rest of his career, Becks has achieved more in his career than most players do in a lifetime.

DID YOU KNOW?

'The Red Devils' were known as Newton Heath until 1902 when the legend Manchester United was born.

FOREST

ALL THE TOP INFO ON ALL YOUR FAVE STARS!

NO.7

PIERRE VAN HOOIJDONK

NOTTM FOR

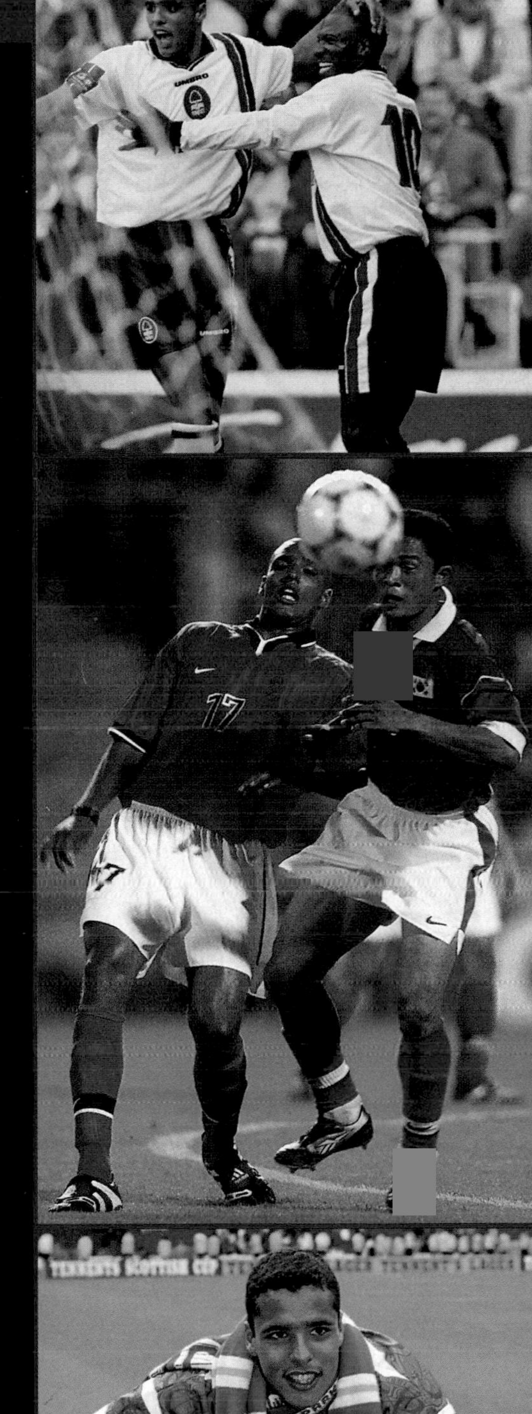

ON LEAVING CELTIC OVER CASH

"What they were offering was good enough for the homeless, but not good enough for an international striker."

ON NOT BEING SIGNED BY ONE OF THE BIG DUTCH CLUBS

"When I was at NAC Breda in Holland Feyenoord showed an interest, but they couldn't afford the fee. Ajax and PSV already had enough strikers, so there was nowhere else to go. To be honest, the attraction of playing for one of those teams is not as big as it was anymore."

ON KEEPING HIS AMAZING GOALSCORING RECORD GOING STRONG

"In my career so far I've always scored a lot of goals. Obviously when you're playing in Scotland or the First Division there's more chances of scoring than in the Premiership, for sure. However, I think we have enough quality to be among the best in this league, so I don't see why not."

ON THE SECRET OF NOTT'M FOREST'S PROMOTION LAST SEASON

"We have a lot of quality players in our team. We have lads who can play the game and pass the ball. If you do that very well, it can make the difference in a lot of games. Despite winning the league, I think we all found it much tougher than we expected."

ON PROVING HIMSELF IN THE PREMIERSHIP

"Yes, I've set my sights on that one for this season. It was a pity two seasons ago that I only played in the last eight games, it was a struggle, although we only lost one. This time I think we're better equipped, but in the end the club has to show real ambition if we want to seriously challenge."

ON BEING IN THE DUTCH WORLD CUP FINALS TEAM

"Yeah, to get in amongst Bergkamp, Kluivert and Hasselbaink was great for me. But to stay at that level I will have to continue to play very well and score a lot of goals. It doesn't matter what country I am playing in, or what division, I have to score goals and play well to stay in contention for a place in the Dutch national squad."

ON BEING IN THE MEDIA SPOTLIGHT

"It doesn't bother me. It's part and parcel of the game these days. When you're young you just want to be successful, so once you get there you have to be grateful and learn how to handle these things. It's so much part of the business and you'll miss it when you hang up your boots."

ON ENGLISH FOOTBALL

"While I think the game is very exciting, it can never challenge the best in Europe. I think players abroad understand tactics better, even at a young level. I think Britain really needs to get rid of school football. We don't have that at all in Holland – youngsters are all taught by proper coaches."

ON WINNING THE SCOTTISH FA CUP WITH CELTIC

"The club were on a real low when I joined and Celtic is a club where the fans find it hard to accept any downs. But after I scored the winner in the cup against Airdrie, I could see how much this club means to its fans. There were as many crying as celebrating."

ON HIS OTHER REASONS FOR LEAVING SCOTLAND

"The main problem was having to play each team four times a season – it drives you mad. And the crowd are always on your back to get forward."

LEAGUE CUP 1994
ASTON VILLA v MAN UTD

MARCH 27th 1994
ASTON VILLA 3-1 MAN UTD (HT: 1-0)

ASTON VILLA: Bosnich, Barrett, Staunton (sub: Cox), Teale, McGrath, Richardson, Daley, Townsend, Saunders, Atkinson, Fenton. Scorers: Atkinson, Saunders (2)
MAN UTD: Sealey; Parker, Irwin, Bruce (sub: McClair), Kanchelskis, Pallister, Cantona, Ince, Keane, Hughes, Giggs (sub: Sharpe). Scorer: Hughes
REFEREE: K. Cooper (Pontypridd)
ATT: 77,231 (At Wembley)

STAR MAN DEAN SAUNDERS

Aston Villa won their first trophy since the 1982 European Cup and succeeded in ending United's dreams of of a unique treble in the process. Dalian Atkinson gave Villa a half-time lead and Dean Saunders added another with 15 minutes remaining. But Mark Hughes gave the United fans hope of a dramatic comeback with a quality strike past Mark Bosnich. As 'The Red Devils' pushed forward in search of an equalizer Villa hit them on the break and won a penalty after Andrei Kanchelskis was sent off for deliberate handball on his own goal-line. Dean Saunders stepped forward and smashed the penalty past former Villa 'keeper Les Sealey.

Man Of The Match Kevin Richardson lifted the trophy for Aston Villa and their boss Ron Atkinson celebrated his third Wembley success as a manager.

MOMENT OF THE MATCH

A 70th minute tackle by Man Of The Match Kevin Richardson robbed United's Lee Sharpe of a certain goal and it proved decisive five minutes later as Villa increased their lead through Welsh hitman Dean Saunders.

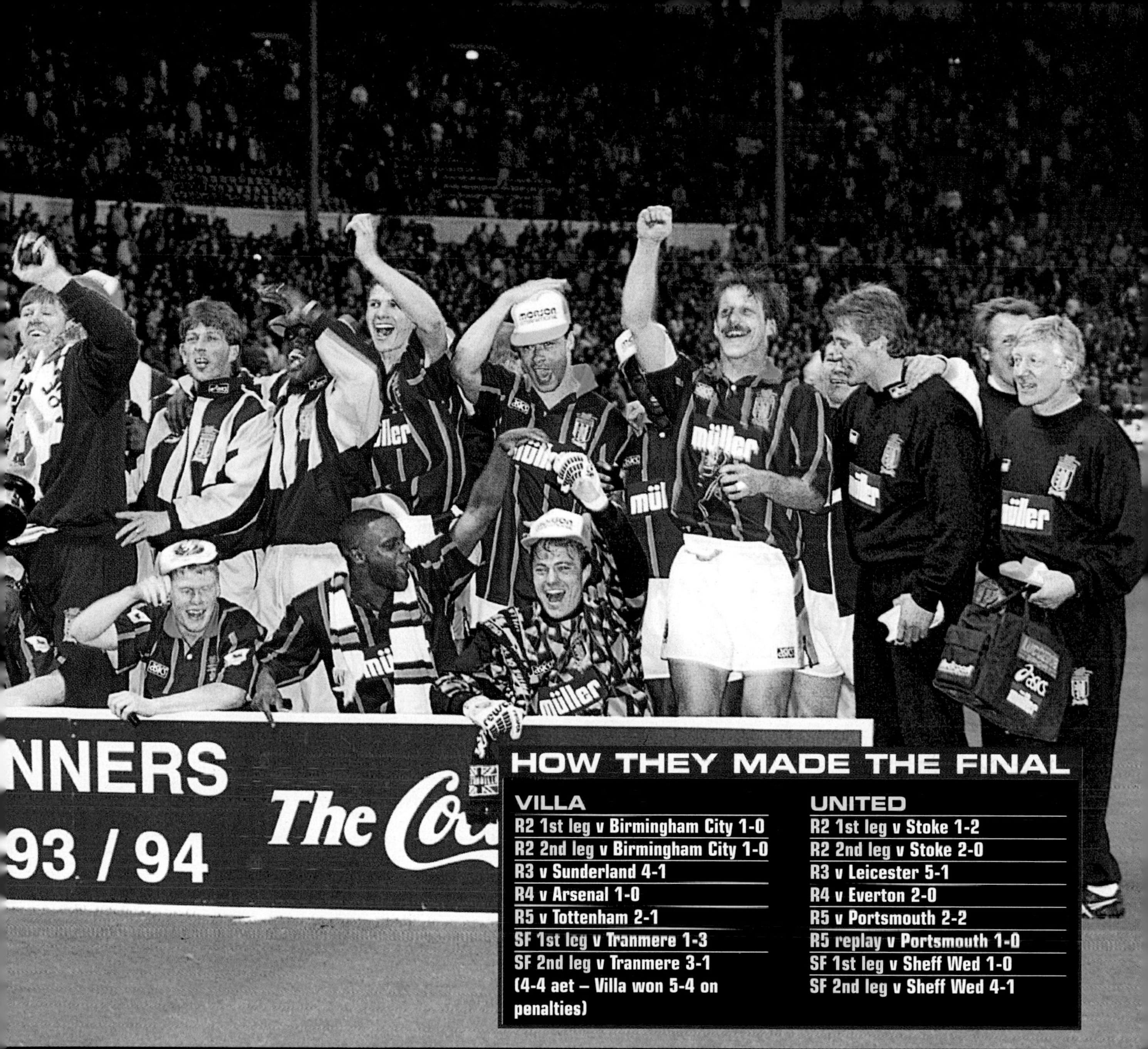

HOW THEY MADE THE FINAL

VILLA	UNITED
R2 1st leg v Birmingham City 1-0	R2 1st leg v Stoke 1-2
R2 2nd leg v Birmingham City 1-0	R2 2nd leg v Stoke 2-0
R3 v Sunderland 4-1	R3 v Leicester 5-1
R4 v Arsenal 1-0	R4 v Everton 2-0
R5 v Tottenham 2-1	R5 v Portsmouth 2-2
SF 1st leg v Tranmere 1-3	R5 replay v Portsmouth 1-0
SF 2nd leg v Tranmere 3-1 (4-4 aet – Villa won 5-4 on penalties)	SF 1st leg v Sheff Wed 1-0
	SF 2nd leg v Sheff Wed 4-1

EVERYTHING YOU WANTED TO KNOW ABOUT

ARSENAL

Arsenal's double triumph last season was a victory for Arsene Wenger's unique blend of an English defence, French midfield and Dutch attack. But it wasn't the first time 'The Gunners' had fired their way to mega-glory. Back in 1971, Arsenal won the double with a side that included George Graham and TV presenter Bob Wilson. Then, as manager, Graham guided the club to a series of trophies in the late 1980s and early 1990s. So if you want the lowdown and don't know your Arsenal from your elbow, read on!

FORMED: 1886
GROUND: Arsenal Stadium, Highbury
NICKNAME: 'The Gunners'
RECORD LEAGUE VICTORY: 12-0 v Loughborough Town March 12th 1900
MOST LEAGUE APPEARANCES: David O'Leary – 558 appearances (1975-93)
MOST CAPPED PLAYER: Kenny Sansom – 77 caps for England.
PLAYER WITH MOST LEAGUE GOALS: Ian Wright – 124 (1991-98)
TOP SCORER 1997/98 (LEAGUE): Dennis Bergkamp 16.

HONOURS: LEAGUE CHAMPIONS: 1930 - 31, 1932 - 33, 1933 - 34, 1934 - 35, 1937 - 1938, 1947 - 48, 1952 - 53, 1970 - 71, 1988 - 89, 1990 - 91, 1997-98. **F.A CUP:** 1930, 1936, 1950, 1971, 1979, 1993, 1998. **DOUBLE:** 1970 -71, 1997 - 98. **LEAGUE CUP:** 1987, 1993 **UEFA CUP:** 1970. **EUROPEAN CUP - WINNERS CUP:** 1994

THE COUNTRY'S BIGGEST CLUBS!

GREAT MANAGER GEORGE GRAHAM

George Graham was part of the famous 1971 double winning Arsenal side, and his midas touch continued into his management reign. In his eight years in charge at Highbury he won no less than six trophies, including two titles and the European Cup Winners' Cup.

WHAT A STAR ARSENAL'S GREAT PLAYERS

TONY ADAMS

Tony Adams collects trophies like Gazza collects extra weight. The Arsenal captain has won the league title three times, the FA Cup twice, the League Cup twice and the European Cup Winners' Cup. Since he made his debut in 1983, Adams has become the rock on which Arsenal are built under George Graham, Bruce Rioch and Arsene Wenger. His left-foot strike in Arsenal's title-clinching 4-0 win v Everton last season summed up the man – a born winner.

DENNIS BERGKAMP

Dennis Bergkamp arrived at Highbury in 1995, with the club still reeling from the dismissal of George Graham. But cometh the hour, cometh the Dutchman and Gunners fans haven't looked back since. He exploded into life last season, scoring goals that took the world's breath away and is a firm fans' favourite at Highbury. Whether its creating chances for his team-mates, or curling his own strikes into the top corner, 'Dennis The Menace' is quite a handful for opposing defences.

LIAM BRADY

Liam Brady is still considered by many to be the best midfielder ever to play at Highbury. 'Chippy' broke into 'The Gunners'' first team in 1973 and his cultured left-foot dominated the Arsenal midfield, creating chance after chance. Brady's talent was noticed when he won the Player Of The Year award in 1979, the same year he guided the side to a dramatic 3-2 FA Cup FInal victory over Man United. He is now back at Highbury working with the youth team.

DID YOU KNOW?

Arsenal tube station on the London Underground was named in honour of the football club in 1932.

SHOOT F.C.

THE SIX-A-SIDE CUP 'MARVIN'S DIARY:'

MARVIN: MIDFIELD

MOXY: FORWARD

POB: DEFENCE

QUARTER FINAL: SHOOT FC V TURNIP FC
WE WON THIS THANKS TO AN INDIVIDUAL GOAL BY MOXY. MIND YOU, THEIR KEEPER MADE A VERY POOR EFFORT TO SAVE IT.

SEMI FINAL: SHOOT FC V BROADCHALKE UNITED
BIT TRICKIER THIS MATCH, WE WERE ONE NIL DOWN AT HALF TIME THEN MENTAL GOT US BACK INTO IT WITH A FREE KICK...

THE KEEPER MADE THE FATAL MISTAKE OF TRYING TO SAVE IT, AND GOT SNAPPED IN TWO FOR HIS TROUBLE. THEY HAD TO PLAY THEIR SUBSTITUTE IN GOAL...

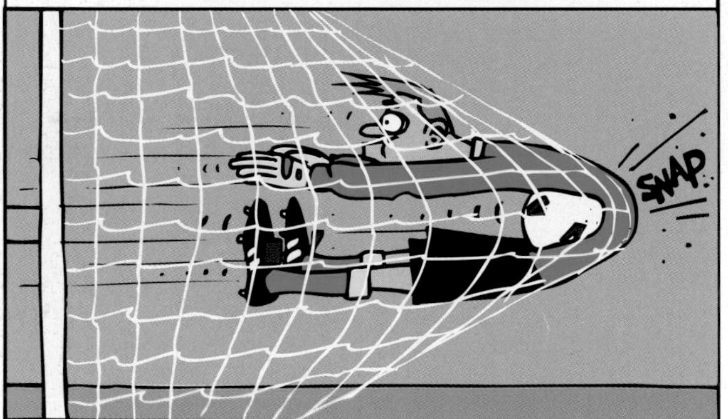

FORTUNATELY HE WAS A BIT OF A DWARF AND I COLLECTED A COUPLE OF SIMPLE HEADERS TO CLINCH IT 3 - 1

THE FINAL: SHOOT FC V SHELTON UGLIES
SO WE GOT TO THE FINAL WHERE WE HAD TO PLAY THE UGLIES WHO HAD A REPUTATION FOR BEING A BIT PHYSICAL....

A WELL DESERVED REPUTATION AS IT TURNED OUT - MOXY TOOK AN ELBOW IN THE FACE!

MENTAL:
DEFENCE

CHECK-OUT:
DEFENCE

KULA:
KEEPER

SCALLY:
SUB.

WE HAD TO BRING ON SCALLY FOR MOXY WHO WAS SERIOUSLY CONFUSED AND DELIRIOUS...

DOWN TO FIVE MEN WITH TWO OF OUR BEST PLAYERS ON THE TOUCH LINE WE WERE REALLY UP AGAINST IT...

FINALLY CHECKOUT GOT HIS £100 TRAXION OUTSOLE PREDATORS WORKING AND DELIVERED A GREAT CROSS....

THEN JUST AS THE HAND OF GOD INTERVENED FOR ARGENTINA SO THE HEAD OF POB INTERVENED FOR US...

AND SO WITH POB'S FIRST EVER GOAL FOR SHOOT FC WE WON THE CUP. EASY, EH..?

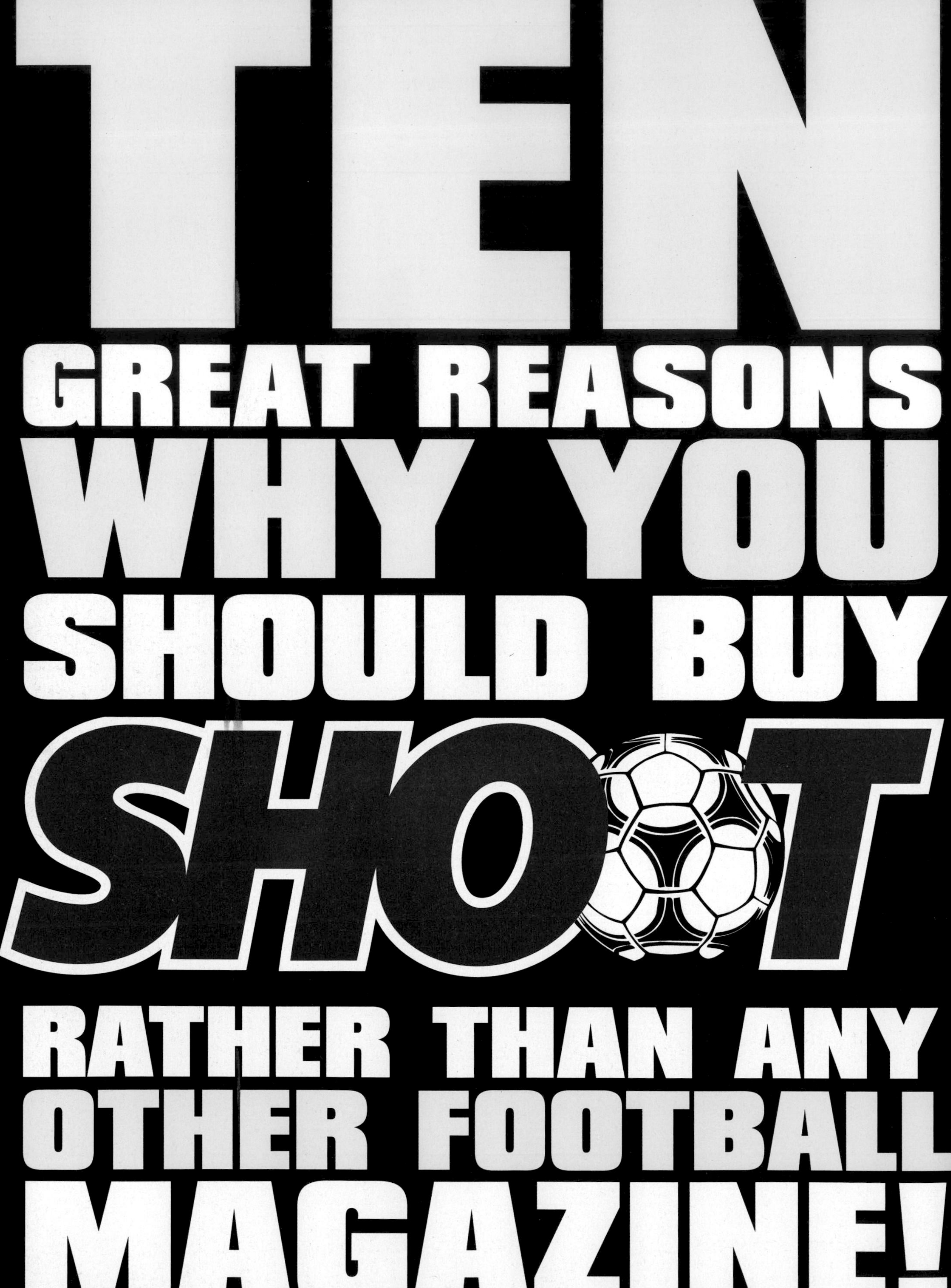
TEN
GREAT REASONS
WHY YOU
SHOULD BUY
SHOOT
RATHER THAN ANY
OTHER FOOTBALL
MAGAZINE!

ALL THE TOP INFO ON ALL YOUR FAVE STARS!

NO.8

SOL CAMPBELL

TOTTENHAM

ON TOTTENHAM'S SUPPORTERS

"I think as long as the fans see you working hard and putting in 100 pre cent effort, then they will appreciate that. Any fans will back players who work hard for the team."

ON PREMIERSHIP DEFENDERS

"There are so many good defenders in the Premiership. They all have different strengths – some are good at tackling, others at passing. For example, Chelsea's Frank Leboeuf is great at spraying the ball around, whereas Tony Adams is a human defensive wall. The game here in this country is much more continental now. You have to think a bit more these days because the game is so fast and bad mistakes are bound to make big headlines."

ON FOREIGNERS IN THE PREMIERSHIP

"The better ones have been great, but I don't think we should have too many because it hinders the progress of the youngsters in this country. They often can't break into a side if a foreign star is already in the team."

ON STAYING FREE OF INJURIES

"You've got to stay focused and do the right things to stay healthy. As long as you stay fit and look after yourself on the pitch, then things will be alright. Don't rush into tackles or dive into challenges that you don't need to. Half the battle is players getting back to match fitness once they're back."

ON COPING WITH PRESSURE

"To a certain extent everyone feels pressure. It's a question of who can handle it, sticking together and fighting it out. You've got to win the battles in the game and let the skill come out – it doesn't work the other way around."

ON ENGLAND BOSS GLENN HODDLE

"I've got to give Mr Hoddle maximum credit, because he has given me a chance and stuck by me. As a technical manager he has helped my control and mastering of the ball a great deal. At international level that is important because the emphasis is always on passing, more so than in the Premiership."

ON PLAYING AT CENTRE-BACK

"Centre back is a very responsible position – you have to do your own job and cover for other people – but you still have to try and relax. Being tense can lead to nerves and nerves can lead to mistakes."

ON BEING VERSATILE AS A PLAYER

"I think it's good for a defender to play in midfield occasionally. It gave me a better understanding of when to play the right passes to the midfield players. You work out very quickly when to pass and when not to. When it looks a bit tight it's not worth the risk, it's better to bypass them. But I definitely prefer playing at the back."

ON THE SPIRIT IN THE ENGLAND CAMP

"The spirit in the squad just gets better all the time, because the lads have gone through an awful lot together. But you've got to respect every team you play, because many countries can play out of their skins if you underestimate them. We don't go out just fearing a few sides, you've got to respect everyone or you'll get caught out."

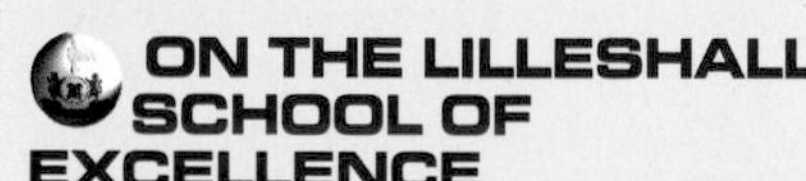

ON THE LILLESHALL SCHOOL OF EXCELLENCE

"I started off there when I was very young. We always did our schoolwork and then played football – it was just brilliant! We often played abroad as well, so I got to see a lot of the world at a young age. The coaches there instilled professionalism into all of us and made it clear how important it is to conduct yourself well off the pitch as well as on it."

ON LAST SEASON'S RELEGATION FIGHT WITH TOTTENHAM

"It wasn't exactly the best season we've had, was it? But everyone at White Hart Lane was confident that we would get out of trouble eventually. It is always difficult when a new manager comes in, and Christian Gross introduced a much more continental approach which took time for many of the players to adjust to. Jurgen Klinnsman obviously came up trumps for us in the end with some important goals, but our injuries didn't help."

UMBRO
ENGLAND
5
5
ENGLAND
UMBRO

FA CUP 1988
WIMBLEDON v LIVERPOOL

MAY 14th 1988
WIMBLEDON 1-0 LIVERPOOL (HT: 1-0)

WIMBLEDON: Beasant; Goodyear, Phelan, Jones, Young, Thorn, Gibson (sub:Scales), Cork (sub:Cunningham), Fashanu, Sanchez, Wise. Scorer: Sanchez
LIVERPOOL: Grobbelaar; Gillespie, Ablett, Nicol, Spackman (sub: Molby), Hansen, Beardsley, Aldridge (sub: Johnston), Houghton, Barnes, McMahon.
REFEREE: B. Hill (Kettering)
ATT: 98,203 (At Wembley)

STAR MAN DAVE BEASANT

'The Crazy Gang' produced the most famous Wembley giantkilling act of all time against a Liverpool side who were already league Champions and were widely expected to blow away their tiny London rivals. Lawrie Sanchez headed the first half winner from a Dennis Wise free-kick and Wimbledon's giant 'keeper Dave Beasant became a double record-breaker. Firstly he became the first 'keeper in history to save a penalty in an FA Cup Final, following his tremendous stop from Liverpool's John Aldridge.

Secondly, as Wimbledon skipper he was also the first goalkeeper to lift the FA Cup. Beasant deserved his Man Of The Match award as the underdogs prevented 'The Reds' from claiming their second double in three years. Sadly 'The Dons' were unable to grace the Cup Winners' Cup with their unique brand of footie magic, as there was a ban on English teams playing in Europe at the time.

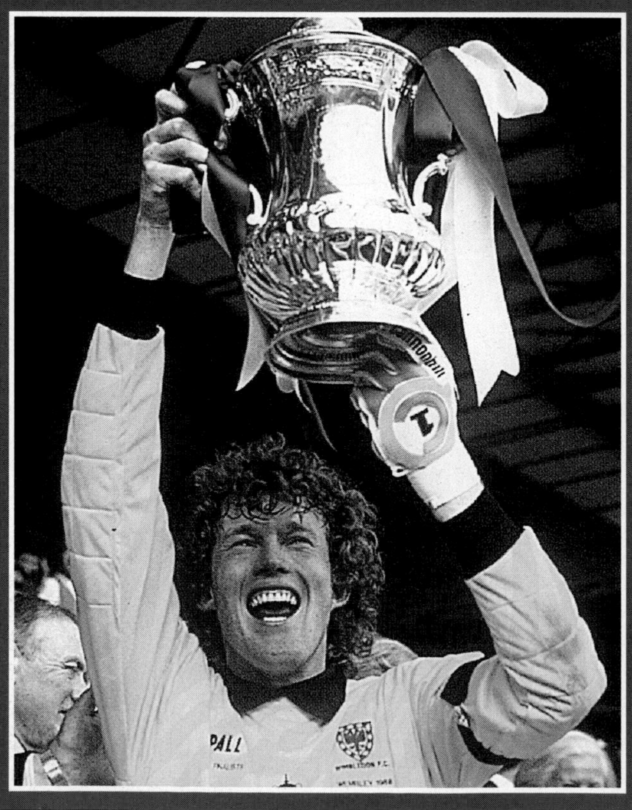

MOMENT OF THE MATCH

John Aldridge had blasted 11 out of 11 successful penalties for Liverpool in the 1988/89 season but Big Dave Beasant launched his huge frame and clawed the ball away from his left-hand post to preserve Wimbledon's lead.

HOW THEY MADE THE FINAL

WIMBLEDON	LIVERPOOL
R3 v West Brom 4-0	R3 v Stoke 0-0
R4 v Mansfield 2-1	R3 replay v Stoke 1-0
R5 v Newcastle 3-1	R4 v Aston Villa 2-0
R6 v Watford 2-1	R5 v Everton 1-0
SF v Luton 2-1	R6 v Man City 4-0
	SF v Nott'm Forest 2-1

EVERYTHING YOU WANTED TO KNOW ABOUT

CHELSEA

Chelsea are back! Completing one half of London's double double last season with their Coca-Cola and European Cup Winners' Cup triumphs, 'The Blues' have emerged from its 27 year long slumber and exploded back into life. Former Juventus star Gianluca Vialli has already shown enormous ambition and ability as a coach and the good times are returning to the fashionable King's Road club at last. Now read all about 'The Blues'' history it in SHOOT's guide to Vialli's victors!

FORMED: 1905
GROUND: Stamford Bridge
NICKNAME: 'The Blues'
RECORD LEAGUE VICTORY: 9-2 v Glossop. September 1st, 1906.
MOST LEAGUE APPEARANCES: Ron Harris – 655 appearances (1962-80).
MOST CAPPED PLAYER: Ray Wilkins – 24 caps for England.
PLAYER WITH MOST LEAGUE GOALS: Bobby Tambling – 164 (1962 - 80)
TOP SCORER 1997/98 (LEAGUE): Gianluca Vialli & Tore Andre Flo 11

HONOURS: LEAGUE CHAMPIONS: 1954-55.
FA CUP 1970; 1997. **LEAGUE CUP:** 1965; 1998.
EUROPEAN CUP WINNERS' CUP: 1971; 1998.

THE COUNTRY'S BIGGEST CLUBS!

GREAT MANAGER RUUD GULLIT

When he lifted the FA Cup in 1997, Ruud Gullit became the first foreign, dreadlocked and black manager to win the famous cup and ended a 27 year barren spell for the club. Sacked controversially last season, he remains very popular at Stamford Bridge.

WHAT A STAR CHELSEA'S GREAT PLAYERS

GIANFRANCO ZOLA

Signed from Parma in 1996 the little Italian scored a series of spectacular goals to ensure him cult status at the Bridge. His tricky, flash skills and glorious goals took Chelsea to the FA Cup Final in his first season with the club and his Semi-Final strike against Wimbledon was out of this world. Last season, he went one better by winning the European Cup Winners' Cup with his second touch of the game after coming on as a late substitute.

DENNIS WISE

'Cheeky', 'cockney' and 'little' are the words usually associated with Dennis Wise, but the words that should be used are 'top' and 'midfielder'. OK, so he is a real character but that shouldn't distract from his ability on the ball and excellent leadership skills. Learning his trade with Wimbledon's Crazy Gang, he even won an FA Cup with them back in 1988. But it's at Stamford Bridge where the little man has really come into his own, leading 'The BLues' to three trophies in two years.

KERRY DIXON

When Kerry Dixon left Chelsea after nine years in 1992, he left behind 147 goals. Kerry had the goalscoring knack and was very much a poacher, not caring how the strikes went in as long they hit the back of the net. Its a wonder he didn't win more than his eight international caps, but then he was competing for a place with master marksman Gary Lineker! Still a cult hero with the Stamford Bridge faithful, Kerry Dixon was a truly lethal marksman.

DID YOU KNOW?

Stamford Bridge was one of the country's leading Greyhound Stadiums in the 1930s.

WHO'S THE GREATEST DEFENDER?

Forwards seem to take all the glory but, more often than not, it's the boys at the back – the defenders – who do all the hard work! But which Premiership stoppers are most capable of striking fear into even the greatest top-flight hitmen? SHOOT finds out.

SOL CAMPBELL TOTTENHAM

AGE: 24

LOWDOWN: One of the best young players in the country, Sol Campbell is also one of the most skillful defenders around. He leads the line at the back with the confidence of one much older, but can also bring the ball out of the defence with power and pace. Cast your mind back to his famous forward run in the World Cup against Colombia if you don't believe us!

STRENGTHS: Sol's a real all-rounder and can play in any position across the backline, making him a unique talent in the British game. He can be equally effective in midfield or up front too! Strength, skills and steel – this man's got them all.

WEAKNESSES: Can be turned by fast strikers and needs to be a bit quicker on his feet.

SHOOT RATING: 98

TONY ADAMS ARSENAL

AGE: 33

LOWDOWN: Big Tony has always been a solid defender, but under Arsenal boss Arsene Wenger and England coach Glenn Hoddle's tuition he's added some real skill to his game. A natural and born leader on the park, Adams just seems to get better and better with age.

STRENGTHS: A solid, skillful tackler, his distribution seems to improve by the match. He may have had his critics down the years but having won the league three times, the FA Cup twice, the League Cup twice and the European Cup Winners' Cup, you can't really knock him can you? He's a real winner!

WEAKNESSES: It is hard to pick fault with a defender like Adams, but he is occasionally shown up by nippy, short attackers.

SHOOT RATING: 95

✪ Each defender is rated out of 100.

GARY NEVILLE MAN UNITED

AGE: 23
LOWDOWN: Although he prefers playing at centre-back, the elder of the most famous brothers in English football has more often appeared at full-back for Man United. But he has played in the middle of defence for England and has never let his country down when called upon.
STRENGTHS: His pace makes him ideal for a more advanced 'wing-back' role and his crossing also suits that position. A clean tackler, he is not the type to let you down in a big game.
WEAKNESSES: His lack of height will always work against him in the centre-back position.
SHOOT RATING:

GARETH SOUTHGATE ASTON VILLA

AGE: 28
LOWDOWN: Forget those naff pizza adverts and that unfortunate miss against the Germans at Euro '96, Southgate is the business. A firm favourite among the Villa Park faithful, his intelligence helps him read the game faster than his opponents. He can also play in midfield or as a sweeper. At 28 he could still appear in another World Cup and is sure to be a vital component in England's Euro 2000 push.
STRENGTHS: Disciplined and skillful, Southgate is also a tough tackler and competitive player. He can deliver telling balls out of defence. His versatility as a player makes him a fine addition to any squad.
WEAKNESSES: Occasionally caught out in the air, he could also do with a bit of extra pace.
SHOOT RATING: 90

RIO FERDINAND WEST HAM

AGE: 20
LOWDOWN: The bright young hope of English football, Rio will be on the international scene for a while yet. Already dubbed 'the next Bobby Moore' after the legendary ex-England captain who led the country to glory at the 1966 World Cup.
STRENGTHS: His skills in bringing the ball out of defence are virtually unrivalled and his pace is pretty handy too! He's good in the air and in the tackle – what more do you want?
WEAKNESSES: Prone to lapses in concentration, Rio also needs to make sure the high hopes the country holds for his career don't weigh him down.
SHOOT RATING: 89

CHRIS PERRY WIMBLEDON

AGE: 25
LOWDOWN: Without doubt the most under-rated defender around, Chris Perry has nevertheless fulfilled his childhood dream by playing for the team he followed as a kid. A dedicated 'Crazy Gang' follower all his life, he now turns on the style for The Dons every Saturday.
STRENGTHS: His composure, balance and pace mean he can cope with the biggest names in the game and he can provide telling long passes to set-up attacks as well. Why hasn't he got an England cap yet? We dunno!
WEAKNESSES: His lack of height is always going to put him at a disadvantage against tall attackers.
SHOOT RATING: 87

FRANK LEBOEUF CHELSEA

AGE: 30
LOWDOWN: One of Ruud Gullit's first signings at Stamford Bridge, Frank has grown in stature in his two years in English football. He is also a World Cup winner with France and is particularly good at going forward for a centre-back. Excellent at free-kicks too.
STRENGTHS: A clean tackler, he can be relied upon in 50/50 challenges. He also has a fantastic knack of setting up attacks with a long pass, or scoring the odd wonder goal himself.
WEAKNESSES: Still suspect when put under strong aerial pressure, he will need to improve that part of his game to truly flourish in English football.
SHOOT RATING: 86

MARTIN KEOWN ARSENAL

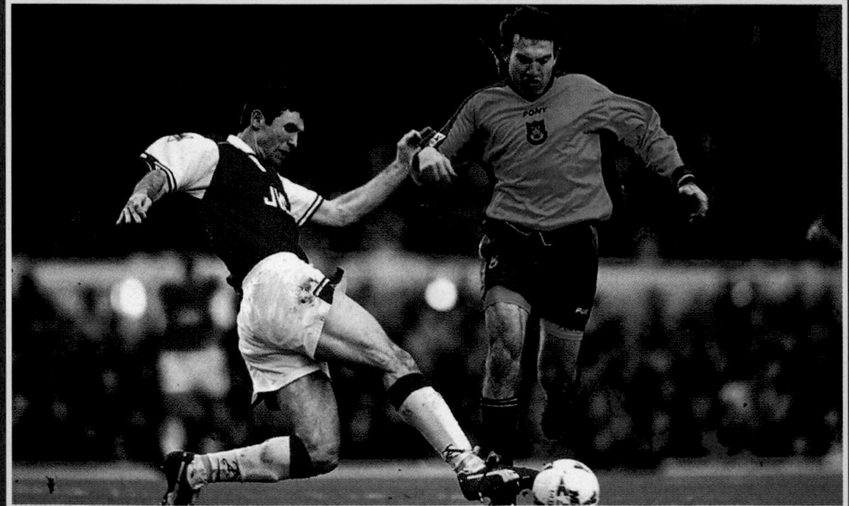

AGE: 32
LOWDOWN: It's impossible not to include more than one Arsenal player in this category and Keown definitely deserves to be the second Gooner in the list. Like Tony Adams, he has improved dramatically under Arsene Wenger, adding some flash skills to his game.
STRENGTHS: One of the quickest players in the game, Keown can keep up with the fastest of Premiership attackers. He is also the greatest man marker in the game by several hundred miles.
WEAKNESSES: Sometimes affected by nerves in the big games, his lapses in concentration have occasionally cost Arsenal dear.
SHOOT RATING: 85

JAAP STAM MAN UNITED

AGE: 25
LOWDOWN: One of the stars of Holland's World Cup campaign, it was a shrewd move by Alex Ferguson to snap him up before the tournament began as his value would have increased by the end of France '98. Currently settling into the English game, he has a bright future ahead of him at Old Trafford.
STRENGTHS: He is a very solid player, who tends to come out of any challenge with the ball at his feet. He is also handy at bringing the ball out of defence and setting up attacks through the midfield.
WEAKNESSES: Sometimes needs too much time on the ball and needs to speed up his game a bit.
SHOOT RATING: 84

COLIN HENDRY BLACKBURN

AGE: 33
LOWDOWN: A traditional 'blood and thunder' centre-half, Colin Hendry doesn't mind mixing it with the toughest of them. Fantastic in the air and on the ground, he was a crucial part of Blackburn's 1995 championship winning team and has served Scotland well also.
STRENGTHS: Sheer guts and determination underpin Hendry's game, and he leads the back line exceptionally well by example. Particularly good in snuffing out players like John Hartson and Duncan Ferguson.
WEAKNESSES: Sometimes his passing lets him down, and can be shown up by tricky attackers like Bergkamp and Zola.
SHOOT RATING: 82

DOMINIC MATTEO LIVERPOOL

AGE: 24
LOWDOWN: He could have made the World Cup Finals if luck had gone more his way. Glenn Hoddle was very interested in the young Anfield star and who can blame him? Adaptable, determined and lightning quick, Matteo is quite a talent!
STRENGTHS: Versatile players are becoming all the more important in today's game and Matteo definitely falls into that category. Defence is one of Liverpool's weaknesses, but with Matteo involved, there is hope for the future.
WEAKNESSES: His head sometimes drops when the chips are down, but has plenty of time to work on that part of his game.
SHOOT RATING: 82

UMBRO
ENGLAND
7
UMBRO
UMBRO

ALL THE TOP INFO ON ALL YOUR FAVE STARS!

NO.9

DAVID BECKHAM

MAN UTD

ON SCORING LOADS OF GREAT GOALS

"I'm always ready to have a go at any time during a game. I think if you see a half chance you have to deal with it. If I think something is on I'll give it a try."

ON PLAYING FOR ENGLAND

"I'm really enjoying my England career. It's a thrill to be part of it all and I feel comfortable in the team. From the first day I came into the squad the manager made me feel at home. There's no nastiness amongst the squad, which is important because it can be intimidating for a young lad. Having some of my Man United mates in the squad helps me a lot too."

ON THE IMPORTANCE OF THE EUROPEAN CUP TO UNITED

"When you look through the history of the club, the European Cup runs all the way through it. That is the one that everybody wants to win. It must have something to do with the team of 1968 that won it so famously. But this is a new era and we'll make our own history."

ON THE UNITED DRESSING ROOM BEFORE A BIG GAME

"We've got a few players at United who like to shout and gee us up, and it's the same with England. I'm the one who likes to sit there and relax a bit more. I've always felt ready for the big internationals because when you're playing for United you get used to the high-pressure games."

ON MAN UNITED'S BRILLIANT FANS

"The support at Old Trafford is amazing, and the noise they make really drives us on. I really think the atmosphere can help to intimidate the opposition players. "

ON GLENN HODDLE

"I'm grateful that Glenn gave me the chance to play for England at such an early age. I've admired him as both a player and as a manager. It's a real honour to be in a team he manages."

ON PLAYING FOR ANOTHER CLUB

"Where else is there to go? It doesn't even enter my head – I love it here at Old Trafford. We've got a great squad and a brilliant manager. Man United is a dream place to play and the supporters are tremendous."

ON THE PRESSURE OF PLAYING IN FRONT OF BIG CROWDS

"To start with it can be quite frightening, but I guess that part and parcel of making it as a pro is being able to handle it. I actually get a big buzz from it and it's the same off the pitch. I used to have to check all the newspapers to see if I'd got a mention, but now I'm in them nearly every day. I get recognised everywhere I go – it can get a bit much at times."

ON UNITED BOSS ALEX FERGUSON

"He's brilliant – he brings through the young players so well. His door is always open, and he always finds the time to speak to you if you need him to. He doesn't expect miracles – he just wants you to work hard and do your best. He gets the best from all his players, and is very protective of them."

ON GETTING STICK FOR SUPPORTING MAN UNITED AS A BOY

"Yeah, I got stick. Obviously living in London there are so many big clubs and most of my mates were Spurs, Arsenal, Chelsea or West Ham fans. But I used to go to school with my United scarf on. No matter how much stick I took, there was no way I was going to change!"

ON BEING CALLED A HOTHEAD

"I control my temper quite well, but people have said I'm hot-headed. I've always reacted to certain things in different ways and maybe in some ways that I've regretted later."

LEAGUE CUP 1993
ARSENAL v SHEFF WED

APRIL 18th 1993
ARSENAL 2-1 SHEFF WED (HT: 1-1)

ARSENAL: Seaman, O' Leary, Winterburn, Parlour, Adams, Linighan, Morrow, Merson, Wright, Campbell, Davis.
Scorers: Merson, Morrow
SHEFF WED: Woods, Nilsson, King (sub: Hyde), Palmer, Anderson, Harkes, Wilson (sub: Hirst), Waddle, Warhurst, Bright, Sheridan. Scorer: Harkes
REFEREE: A. Gunn (Sussex)
ATT: 74,007 (At Wembley)

STAR MAN PAUL MERSON

Paul Merson won the Man Of The Match award which completed a memorable week after his wife had given birth to their second child a few days before the Wembley showdown. John Harkes became the first American to score at Wembley when he fired the Owls ahead in the 10th minute. However, it took Arsenal just eight minutes to reply when a well-worked free-kick ended saw Merse smashing the ball past Wednesday 'keeper Chris Woods.

Steve Morrow was Arsenal's matchwinner with his first goal for the club, after a surging run and cross, again from the energetic Paul Merson. The Arsenal star was even having to play through the pain barrier after his pelvis had popped out following a clash with Wednesday midfielder Danny Wilson. Sadly, Morrow was unable to climb the famous Wembley steps to collect his medal as he broke his left arm in a freak accident during the celebrations af ter the final whistle.

MOMENT OF THE MATCH

Arsenal's equalizer in which Man Of The Match Paul Merson's swerving volley from outside the box rocketed past 'keeper Chris Woods' despairing dive.

ARSENAL

SHEFF WED

Winners 1992/93

HOW THEY MADE THE FINAL

ARSENAL	SHEFF WED
R2 1st leg v Millwall 1-1	R2 1st leg v Hartlepool 3-0
R2 2nd leg v Millwall 1-1	R2 2nd leg v Hartlepool 2-2
aet: Arsenal won 3-1 on penalties	R3 v Leicester 7-1
R3 v Derby 1-1	R4 v QPR 4-0
R3 replay v Derby 2-1	R5 v Ipswich 1-1
R4 v Scarborough 1-0	R5 replay v Ipswich 1-0
R5 v Nott'm Forest 2-0	SF 1st leg v Blackburn 4-2
SF 1st leg v C Palace 3-1	SF 2nd leg v Blackburn 2-1
SF 2nd leg v C Palace 2-0	

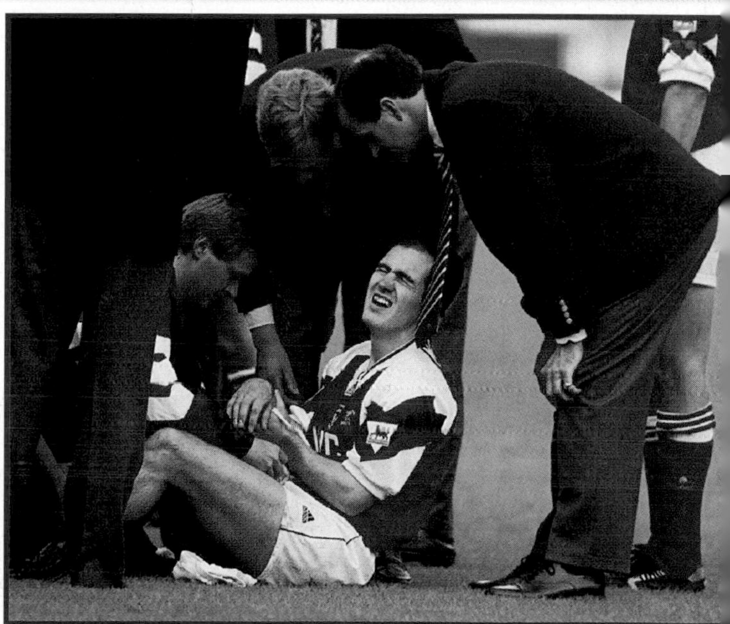

EVERYTHING YOU WANTED TO KNOW ABOUT NEWCASTLE

NEWCASTLE UNITED

Newcastle have finished runners-up in the league twice in the last three years, and came out second best in last season's FA Cup as well. But they remain one of England's most prestigious clubs thanks to their fanatical supporters and league successes at the beginning of the century. For the full lowdown on the Toon army, and to find out why Kevin Keegan will never be forgotten at St James's Park, check out this fantastic full colour guide to the black 'n' white army!

FORMED: 1881
GROUND: St James Park
NICKNAME: 'The Magpies'
RECORD LEAGUE VICTORY: 13-0 v Newport County 5th October 1946.
MOST LEAGUE APPEARANCES: Jim Lawrence – 432 appearances (1904-1922).
MOST CAPPED PLAYER: Alf McMichael – 40 caps for Northern Ireland.
PLAYER WITH MOST LEAGUE GOALS: Jackie Milburn – 177 (1946-1957)
TOP SCORER 1997/98 (LEAGUE): John Barnes 6

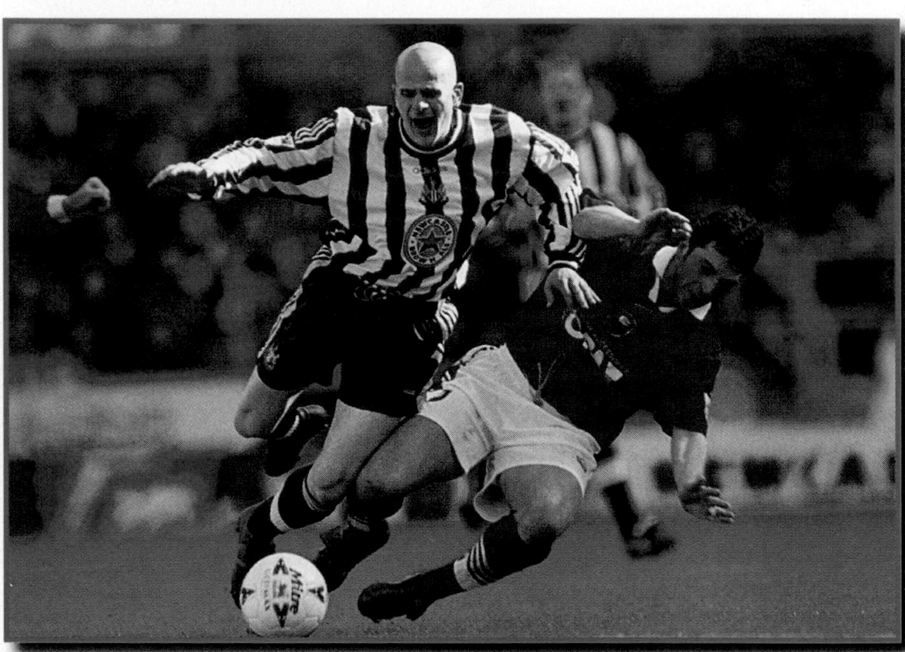

HONOURS: LEAGUE CHAMPIONS: 1904-05; 1906-07; 1908-09; 1926-27. **FA CUP:** 1910; 1924; 1932; 1951; 1952; 1955. **UEFA CUP:** 1969.

THE COUNTRY'S BIGGEST CLUBS!

GREAT MANAGER KEVIN KEEGAN

Kevin was already a superstar when he returned to Tyneside as manager in 1992. He won the Division One title in 1993 and their attacking football took the club within a whisker of the Premiership title in 1996. That attractive football is still missed by the Toon Army.

WHAT A STAR NEWCASTLE'S GREAT PLAYERS

ANDY COLE

He arrived at Newcastle in 1993 from Bristol City and notched 12 goals in his first 11 games. Cole won the Young Player Of The Award in 1994 and had scored a total of 68 goals for 'The Magpies' in just 84 games before Manchester United paid a record £7million for him in 1995. Although his goalscoring record has dipped at Old Trafford, he was known as 'Cole The Goal' at St James's Park such was his lethal touch in the penalty box.

ALAN SHEARER

What more can be said about the goalscoring talent of Alan Shearer? Signed for a world record fee of £15million from Blackburn after he was leading scorer at Euro '96, he has knocked in plenty of strikes for Newcastle despite suffering from injuries. He won the PFA Player Of The Year Award in 1997 and is one of Europe's hottest properties. He could take his pick from any European club if he fanicd a move, but Toon fans will pray he stays at the club he supported as a boy.

ROB LEE

A midfielder with a strong eye for goal, captain Rob Lee is essential to the Newcastle team. Scoring ten goals in his first season at the club, after moving from Charlton, he has a credible goal return for a midfielder. His trademark breaks into the box end up in a goal more often than not, but he has shown versatility as well, by playing at right-back and on the right-wing. Also an experienced international talent, Rob is lover-lee in the eyes of Toon fans!

DID YOU KNOW?

When Steve Watson played for Newcastle against Wolves in 1990 he was just 16 years and 223 days – the club's youngest ever player!

WHO'S THE GREATEST MIDFIELDER?

He may have got sent off for England against Argentina but we still reckon Becks is the best midfielder in the Premiership! But how do other top stars such as Marc Overmars, Dennis Wise and Paul Ince rate against him? SHOOT reveals all!

DAVID BECKHAM MAN UNITED

AGE: 23

LOWDOWN: The story gets more remarkable by the day. Just when we thought Becks had the world at his feet, the fairy story turned sour following a moment of madness in France. Fortunately, with youth on his side, he had the chance to put his error behind him and bounce back.

STRENGTHS: A fantastic eye for goal, a useful crosser of the ball and excellent passer from the middle of the park. When Beckham's about, there will be no shortage of goals. Superb from dead balls as well.

WEAKNESSES: His temperament, suspect even before France '98, is now open to question. Sadly for Becks, he can expect even more provocation than ever.

SHOOT RATING: 98

PATRICK VIEIRA ARSENAL

AGE: 22

LOWDOWN: When he arrived from the AC Milan substitute's bench as Arsene Wenger's first signing, little was known about the lanky French star. But he immediately made an impact and last season formed the strongest midfield partnership in the Premiership with fellow countryman Emmanuel Petit as Arsenal won the double.

STRENGTHS: His athletic build helps him move from box-to-box quickly and win tackles that others would lose.

WEAKNESSES: Occasionally loses his rag and needs to address his temperament. Gunners fans would also like to see him go for goal more.

SHOOT RATING: 97

✪ Each midfielder is rated out of 100.

ROY KEANE MAN UNITED

AGE: 27
LOWDOWN: He missed most of last season through injury, and Man United certainly missed him. Not the most popular man outside of Old Trafford, Keano is loved by Reds fans for his tigerish determination.
STRENGTHS: Courage and guts. He may not be your favourite player, but if you had to fight a war, who else would you rather have at your side. Gary Lineker? Thought not – and Keane can find the net as well.
WEAKNESSES: The obvious flip-side of all that fire in his belly is that Keane's enthusiasm sometimes boils over into petulance and dirty play.
SHOOT RATING: 95

MARC OVERMARS ARSENAL

AGE: 25
LOWDOWN: After a mixed start to his Premiership career, Dutchman Overmars really found his form during the run-in to Arsenal's double winning season. Crucial goals, including the winner at Old Trafford, showed he has the temperament for big games. His pace is virtually unrivalled in England and even when he is double marked, he can still destroy defences.
STRENGTHS: A genuine two-footed player, Overmars can out sprint even the quickest defenders, and his adaptability means he can move up front when needed. He also has a relaxed temperament, so doesn't rise to provocation.
WEAKNESSES: Not the most eager of tacklers and he is occasionally intimidated by heavy challenges or rough play.
SHOOT RATING: 94

PAUL INCE LIVERPOOL

AGE: 31
LOWDOWN: Following a mixed spell in Italy, 'The Guvnor' returned to the Prem to add steel to the Liverpool midfield. His no nonsense tackling and never say die spirit, made him a valuable addition to 'The Reds" squad and he settled back quickly. A national hero for his England form, the image of him bandaged up in Rome is more representative than his unfortunate penalty miss in France.
STRENGTHS: Sheer inspiration. Ince doesn't tolerate failure well and is a true competitor. Would you fancy coming up against him in a 50/50 tackle?
WEAKNESSES: His goal return could be bigger and he sometimes loses his cool.
SHOOT RATING: 91

DARREN ANDERTON TOTTENHAM

AGE: 26

LOWDOWN: Although plagued by well documented injury problems, Anderton remains one of the most creative midfielders in England. His performances in France '98 made his many critics eat their words and Spurs fans will be hoping for a domestic encore of that form.

STRENGTHS: Darren can play in the middle of the park or out wide. From the middle he can split open defences with telling passes, while on the flanks his athleticism takes him into areas where he can provide quality crosses.

WEAKNESSES: Well, what do you think? 'Sicknote' would get injured making a sandwich and is the only player who has had to leave the field during a vital World Cup game to find his lost contact lens!

SHOOT RATING: 90

PAUL MERSON MIDDLESBROUGH

AGE: 30

LOWDOWN: After his much publicised problems off the field and the heartbreak of being rejected by his beloved Arsenal, it's incredible that 'The Magic Man' has come back stronger than ever with Boro. Playing in his favoured attacking role, he was the main factor behind Boro's promotion and Coca-Cola Cup Final appearance last season. He also made an effective, if short, contribution to England's France '98 campaign.

STRENGTHS: Any player who can create and score goals in equal measure is worth his weight in gold. The Merse is also a determined, level-headed character whose experience is of enormous help to his team-mates.

WEAKNESSES: Prefers to cut inside and shoot, where a sprint down the flanks followed by a killer cross would sometimes be more effective.

SHOOT RATING: 88

MATT LE TISSIER SOUTHAMPTON

AGE: 30

LOWDOWN: It would be a terrible shame if Le Tissier were to be remembered for his lack of international experience, rather than the sublime skills he has shown throughout his club career. Season after season, he has dominated Goal Of The Month competitions and he can set them up for his team-mates as well.

STRENGTHS: Wonder goals. We all have our personal favourites but what we all agree on is that Matt Le Tiss is not a tap-in man. Fantastic from dead balls as well.

WEAKNESSES: Tends to drift in and out of games, doesn't get involved in any defensive work and question marks hang over his ambition.

SHOOT RATING: 87

DAVID BATTY NEWCASTLE

AGE: 30
LOWDOWN: Forget the penalty miss, David Batty is a real winner. During his time at Leeds and Blackburn, he has tasted success and demands nothing but 100 per cent commitment from himself and his team-mates.
STRENGTHS: He doesn't muck about when it comes to the tackle, does he? Batty is ferocious in the challenge and motors from box to box like the greatest midfielders must. He can also find the net from time to time as well.
WEAKNESSES: OK, remember that penalty miss then! He is also prone to boiling over and lashing out. Red cards don't help your team-mates much, do they?
SHOOT RATING: 85

ROBBIE EARLE WIMBLEDON

AGE: 33
LOWDOWN: One of the most celebrated players to be overlooked by Glenn Hoddle, England's loss was Jamaica's gain as Earle played a starring role in 'The Reggae Boys" World Cup journey. His box-to-box runs are legendary.
STRENGTHS: Earle has had a fantastic goal return throughout his career, but he can often be found at the other end of the pitch making up the numbers in defence as well.
WEAKNESSES: If we were being ultra critical we could point to his lack of tackling, but that's not really his role is it?
SHOOT RATING: 84

DENNIS WISE CHELSEA

AGE: 32
LOWDOWN: He's won the European Cup Winners' Cup, the League Cup and the FA Cup twice, yet he wasn't needed for England's France '98 campaign. Fortunately for little Dennis, the Chelsea fans are no fools and they know a top midfielder when they see one.
STRENGTHS: His blend of skill and steel is as effective as it is rare in the top-flight nowadays. He can play wide on the right and in the middle of the park, and his dead ball deliveries are telling. He's also a natural leader.
WEAKNESSES: Occasionally gets involved in stupid confrontations and needs to calm down a bit.
SHOOT RATING: 82

ALL THE TOP INFO ON ALL YOUR FAVE STARS!

NO.10

ALAN SHEARER

NEWCASTLE

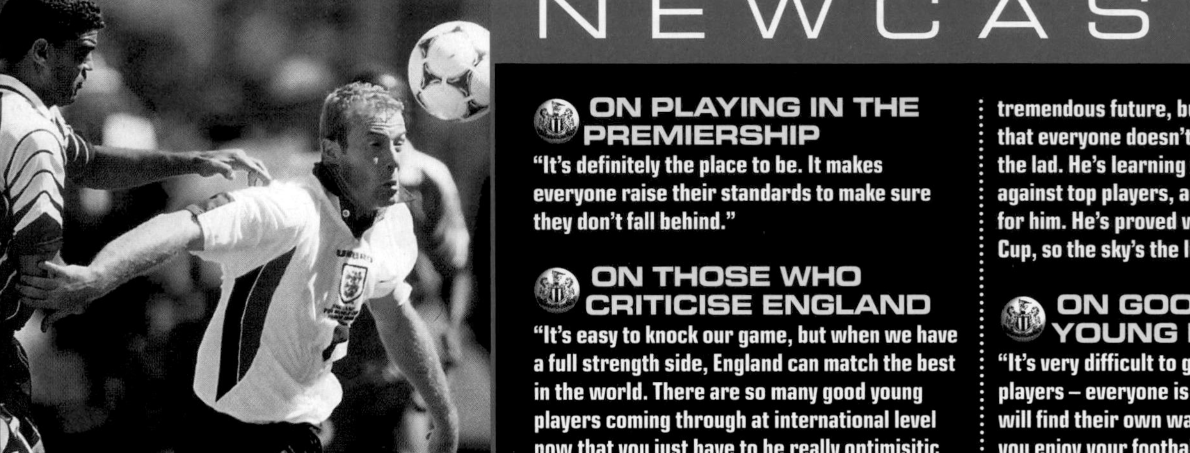

ON PLAYING IN THE PREMIERSHIP

"It's definitely the place to be. It makes everyone raise their standards to make sure they don't fall behind."

ON THOSE WHO CRITICISE ENGLAND

"It's easy to knock our game, but when we have a full strength side, England can match the best in the world. There are so many good young players coming through at international level now that you just have to be really optimisitic for the future."

ON HIS NEED FOR A BIT OF PRIVACY

"I've got to have my privacy just like everyone else. I'm lucky enough to have a good family life and people respect that. I can't go to the supermarket, but then I think that's one of the advantages! I would never moan about being famous because the advantages far outweigh the disadvantages. I think you just learn to live with it and cope with it. The main problem is not being able to take the kids where I'd like to go."

ON PICKING UP SERIOUS INJURIES

"In December 1992 I did my cruciate knee ligaments and a lot of people wrote me off. Some said I'd never play again, but after nine months I was back at full strength. In April 1996, I had a groin injury that needed an operation, but I was back after a month. Then to get an ankle injury in August1997 was a major setback, but hopefully I can steer clear of them from now on."

ON QUICK RECOVERIES

"I think I'm a good healer. Even though I've had serious injuries I'm always able to come back quicker than people expect. The frustration of not being out there playing can be much more painful than the actual injury itself, to be honest with you."

ON MICHAEL OWEN

"He looks like he's going to have a tremendous future, but I think it's important that everyone doesn't put too much pressure on the lad. He's learning from playing alongside and against top players, and that can only be good for him. He's proved what he can do in the World Cup, so the sky's the limit for him now."

ON GOOD ADVICE TO YOUNG PLAYERS

"It's very difficult to give advice to young players – everyone is different and everyone will find their own way. All I'd say is make sure you enjoy your football – if you're not enjoying it you shouldn't be playing. There's no way you'll make it if you don't love the game."

ON MISSING ENGLAND GAMES

"I don't like missing any England games, particularly when I'm fit. But there's such fierce competition for attacking positions and the manager needs a chance to look at everyone. You only have to look at the players who aren't in the England squad to see how difficult it is for the England boss."

ON SCORING GOALS FOR ENGLAND AND NEWCASTLE UNITED

"Obviously, it's great. But the credit should also go to my team-mates because without good service I wouldn't be able to do it. I just play because I love football. I do get paid well, but that comes with being a top footballer. I love winning."

ON MATCHING THE BEST TEAMS IN THE WORLD

"It gives everyone involved the added confidence and added belief that you have achieved something. We've beaten the best over recent years, although to lose to Brazil at Le Tournoi and to Argentina in the World Cup was no disgrace. They've both been among the world's best sides for as long as I can remember."

CLASSIC CUP FINALS

EUROPEAN CUP-WINNERS' CUP 1991
MAN UTD v BARCELONA

MAY 15th 1991
MAN UTD 2-1 BARCELONA (HT: 0-0)

MANCHESTER UNITED: Sealey, Irwin, Blackmore, Bruce, Phelan, Pallister, Robson, Ince, McClair, Hughes, Sharpe. **Scorers:** Hughes (2)
BARCELONA: Busquets, Nando, Alexanco (sub: Pinilla), Koeman, Ferrer, Bakero, Goicoechea, Eusebio, Salinas, Laudrup, Beguiristain. **Scorer:** Koeman
REFEREE: Karlsson (Sweden).
ATT: 45,000 (in Rotterdam)

STAR MAN MARK HUGHES

Manchester United made it a triumphant return for English clubs in European competition when they beat the mighty Spainsh giants Barcelona to lift the European Cup Winners' Cup in Rotterdam. Former Barcelona player Mark Hughes was the hero as he scored both United's goals. The opening strike came in the 68th minute after an expertly floated free-kick from 'Captain Marvel' Bryan Robson was headed on by Steve Bruce and 'Sparky' got the final touch.

United added a second seven minutes later when Hughes went past the Barca keeper and squeezed the ball into the net from the narrowest of angles. There were a nervous last 10 minutes for 'The Red Devils' after Ronald Koeman powered a 30 yard free-kick past Les Sealey in the United goal. However, once Barca were reduced to 10 men following the sending-off of defender Nando there was no doubt over the outcome as United deservedly claimed their second European trophy.

MOMENT OF THE MATCH

Following a delightful chip from Bryan Robson, Hughes belted the ball into the net from a tight angle to put United two up and on course to be the first British team to win a European trophy in six years.

HOW THEY MADE THE FINAL

UNITED	BARCELONA
R1 1st leg v Pecsi Munkas 2-0	R1 1st leg v Trabzonspor 0-1
R1 2nd leg v Pecsi Munkas 1-0	R1 2nd leg v Trabzonspor 7-2
R2 1st leg v Wrexham 3-0	R2 1st leg v Fram 2-1
R2 2nd leg v Wrexham 2-0	R2 2nd leg v Fram 3-0
QF 1st leg v Montpellier 1-1	QF 1st leg v Kiev Dynamo 3-2
QF 2nd leg v Montpellier 2-0	QF 2nd leg v Kiev Dynamo 1-1
SF 1st leg v Legia Warsaw 3-1	SF 1st leg v Juventus 3-1
SF 2nd leg v Legia Warsaw 1-1	SF 2nd leg v Juventus 0-1

EVERYTHING YOU WANTED TO KNOW ABOUT

LIVERPOOL

Even though they've not won a lot recently, 'The Reds' remain England's most successful side ever. While Man United and Arsenal may have dominated recent years, the league title has been won by the Anfield aces a record 18 times. WIth a fit Robbie Fowler rejoining Michael Owen in attack, a return to the good times could be just around the corner for the red half of Merseyside. So if you want to know about their glorious past, and exciting present, read on for a full SHOOT lowdown

FORMED: 1892
GROUND: Anfield
NICKNAME: 'The Reds'
RECORD LEAGUE VICTORY: 10-1 v Rotherham Town February 18th, 1896.
MOST LEAGUE APPEARANCES: Ian Callaghan – 640 (1960-1978)
MOST CAPPED PLAYER: Ian Rush – 67 caps for Wales.
PLAYER WITH MOST LEAGUE GOALS: Roger Hunt – 245 (1959-69)
TOP SCORER 1997/98 (LEAGUE): Michael Owen 18

HONOURS: LEAGUE CHAMPIONS: 1900-01; 1905-06; 1921-22; 1922-23; 1946-47; 1963-64; 1965-66; 1972-73; 1975-76; 1976-77; 1978-79; 1979-80; 1981-82; 1982-83; 1983-84; 1985-86; 1987-88; 1989-1990. **FA CUP:** 1965; 1974; 1986; 1989; 1992. **LEAGUE & FA CUP DOUBLE:** 1985-86. **LEAGUE CUP:** 1981; 1982; 1983; 1984; 1995. **EUROPEAN CUP:** 1977; 1978; 1981; 1984. **UEFA CUP:** 1973; 1976. **EUROPEAN SUPER CUP WINNERS:** 1977.

GREAT MANAGER KENNY DALGLISH

King Kenny, as he's known at Anfield, has starred for the club as both player and manager. He led 'Pool to three title and two FA Cup Finals. That record remains a weight on the shoulders of the current regime and the benchmark for them to live up to.

WHAT A STAR LIVERPOOL'S GREAT PLAYERS

ALAN HANSEN

BBC footie pundit Alan Hansen might spend every Saturday night criticising defences, but he's entitled to as he was the star of a fantastic Liverpool back four for almost a decade and a half. The tall, graceful Scot was signed from Partick Thistle in 1977 and won 16 major honours before his illustrious career was ended by a persistent knee injury in 1991. Hansen is still a popular figure at Anfield and is assured of a place in the history books.

JOHN BARNES

Barnes was one of the finest England strikers in the 1980s. Liverpool signed him from Watford in 1987 and a year later he had won the Player Of The Year Award. His dazzling wing play steered Liverpool to the championship in 1987-88 and 1989-90. He lifted the Coca-Cola Cup for Liverpool in 1995 before joining Newcastle United on a free transfer in August 1997. Currently in the twilight of his career, it would be no surprise if he returned to Anfield in a coaching capacity in the near future.

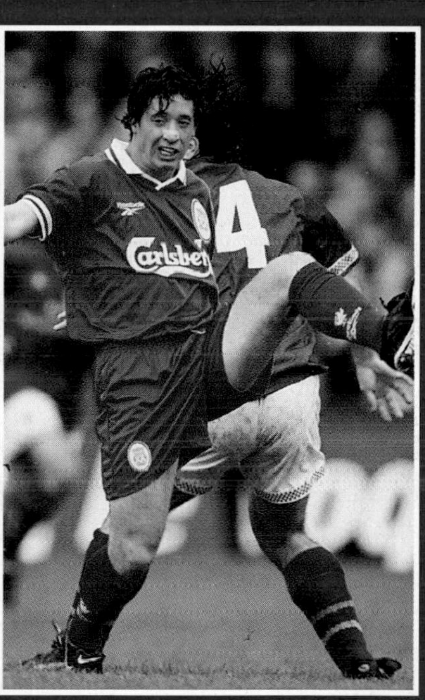

ROBBIE FOWLER

Lethal, accurate and skillful, Robbie Fowler scares the life out of opposing defenders. A product of the Liverpool youth ranks Fowler made his senior debut as an 18-year-old in the League Cup at Fulham. He gave notice of what was to come when he scored five goals in the return leg at Anfield. By December 1996 he had scored 100 goals in 165 games, reaching his century even faster than Liverpool's other strike master Ian Rush.

DID YOU KNOW?

Former boss Bill Shankly preferred to stand on the Kop after his retirement in 1974 than watch matches from the stands.

He was a bit

GEORGE BEST

Often described in glowing terms as one of the most naturally talented individuals ever to grace a football field. The slight Belfast lad joined Man United as a homesick 15-year-old and under the careful guidance of manager Matt Busby quickly made the grade into top-flight professional football as a 17-year-old. The year was 1963.

The following year he was playing international football and before he was 20 he'd won his first league title medal. His success was based on incredible balance, pace and a deadly accuracy in front of goal. He could leave opponents for dead with a dazzling array of skills – dribbling, nutmegging, shimmying – and could tackle like a fullback.

Best's most glorious moment with United came in 1968 when they became the first English club to win the European Cup. He was also named European Footballer Of The Year. For several years it seemed that there was no limit to what the gifted young Irishman could achieve.

Sadly, Best's hectic social life and huge fame eventually caught up with him and his career nosedived in the early '70s as United battled relegation and he battled alcoholism. He drifted out of top level football at 27 and retired in 1983.

MODERN DAY EQUIVALENT: Ryan Giggs with the attitude of Stan Collymore.

HOW MUCH WOULD HE BE WORTH NOW? £30million

GORDON BANKS

Sheffield born (1937) Banks is generally regarded as a strong candidate for the greatest 'keeper of all time title, thanks to a distinguished international career in which he won 73 caps, as well as the World Cup.

He began his career slowly but solidly. His four years at small town Chesterfield stood him in good stead, before moving onto unfashionable Leicester City. He won few honours at Filbert Street, but was still singled out by England boss Alf Ramsey, making his country's No.1 jersey his own between 1966 and 1972.

No-one is quite sure what made him stand out, but it's fair to say that he simply made things look easy and had the respect of all his players.

The most talked about moment in his career is the astonishing save Banks made against Pele in the 1970 Mexico World Cup. Pele was moved enough to say: "At that moment I hated Gordon Banks more than any man in soccer," but he later admitted, "It was the greatest save I have ever seen."

Sadly, Gordon's career at the top was cruelly cut short at 35 after losing the sight in his right eye following a car crash. But he nevertheless set a benchmark in the British game which all current and future 'keepers are measured by. His long-term understudy in the England team, Peter Shilton, went on to win 125 caps.

MODERN DAY EQUIVALENT: David Seaman – but even better.

HOW MUCH WOULD HE BE WORTH NOW? £10million

KENNY DALGLISH

As one fan's banner pointed out, 'Kenny's from heaven'! The wee Scotsman started his career at Celtic in 1970, and very quickly began to establish himself as an indespensible figure in any team thanks to his all round ability.

He signed for Liverpool in 1977 as a replacement for Kevin Keegan, and later moved the club's chairman, John Smith, to describe him as the best player the Merseyside giants had signed in the 20th century! King Kenny, as he became known, was a vital figure for 'The Reds', helping them dominate European and English football for well over a decade.

There is barely a domestic trophy that Dalglish has not won twice, but sadly the international picture tells a different story. Despite winning 102 caps for Scotland, he did not always reproduce his club form for his country.

Kenny's success as a player continued as a boss with Liverpool and Blackburn, but he's yet to win anything with current club Newcastle.

MODERN DAY EQUIVALENT: Paul Scholes

HOW MUCH WOULD HE BE WORTH NOW? £12million

special

SHOOT REMEMBERS SOME OF FOOTIE'S GREATEST EVER STARS!

PELE

Another candidate for the 'most talented footballer ever' prize. A star from the word go, the little Brazillian rose to the top thanks to a lethal cocktail of unsurpassed control, speed, and deadliness in front of goal – being able to shoot with either foot.

Scored on his club debut at the age of 16 and did the same when making his international debut the following year. Initially gained a reputation as a reckless hothead, but quickly learned to control the negative sides of his game.

1958 saw Pele burst onto the world stage as an inside forward in the first of his four World Cup tournaments. Brazil

clinched the title, with the 17 year old grabbing six goals in the tournament. He went on to score 1,283 first class goals during his club career, which was largely spent with Santos of Brazil. He hung up his international boots at just 31, having scored 97 goals in 111 matches.

For Pele, football was and still is a love affair: "Football is like a religion to me. I worship the ball and treat it like a God," he once said.

MODERN DAY EQUIVALENT: Ronaldo

HOW MUCH WOULD HE BE WORTH NOW? Talent like Pele's comes along once in a lifetime – he's priceless!

DIEGO MARADONA

Wayward Argentinian genius who was universally acclaimed as the best attacking player on the planet during his peak years in the 1980s. However, while Pele received love and respect for his skills and affable attitude, Maradona's aloofness and arrogance did not endear him to crowds.

On the pitch, no-one else was capable of the instant control, dribbling skills, and turn of pace that he used to such stunning effect. It was ironic that Diego's finest hours for Argentina at the World Cup in 1986 have been best remembered for the cheeky 'Hand Of God' goal he scored in the Quarter-Final against England, rather than his stunning individual effort in the same game.

Meanwhile, his status at club level rose to almost god-like proportions with Italian side Napoli. Maradona inspired them to two league titles during his seven years at the club.

The '90s has been a decade Maradona will want to forget, with drugs, injury and loss of form ending a brilliant career.

MODERN DAY EQUIVALENT: No-one – he's a total one-off!

HOW MUCH WOULD HE BE WORTH NOW? £40million

FERENC PUSKAS

Incredible as it may seem, during the '50s Hungary produced some of the most feared international teams ever seen in Europe.

Hungary's best player from those times was Puskas, or the 'Galloping Major', as he was known by the British press.

The striker made his debut for Hungary in 1945 at the age of 19. He proceeded to terrorise defences, finishing with 50 goals in the Hungarian league championship of 1948. The year after winning gold at the Olympics, the Hungarian team captained by Puskas visited 'invincible' England at Wembley and thumped them 6-3!

Puskas went on to score 83 goals in 84 games for Hungary, an international goal tally has only been bettered by Pele.

MODERN DAY EQUIVALENT: Christian Vieri

HOW MUCH WOULD HE BE WORTH NOW? £18million

JOHAN CRUYFF

The tempermental Dutchman (born in Amsterdam in 1947) earned his place among the world's elite during the late '60s and '70s as a natural goalscorer blessed with superb ball control, balance and acceleration.

Cruyff's roots lie near the ground of Ajax Amsterdam, and the youngsters obvious talents were spotted at the tender age of 10, where he worked his way up through Ajax's youth system, finally making his professional debut as an 18-year-old.

He was awarded the European Footballer Of The Year title three times as part of the supremely successful Ajax side of the early '70s, winning several European Cups and regularly finishing the top scorer in the Dutch league.

As captain of Holland, Cryuff narrowly missed out on what would have been his ultimate acheivement – a World Cup winners medal in 1974.

His international statistics tell their own story: 33 goals in 48 appearances. From Ajax he transferred to Barcelona in a then world record fee of £922,000 before retiring at the top at just 31.

Cruyff was later tempted out of retirement, but was soon lured into a coaching role at former club Ajax and later Barcelona. Largely due to his 40-a-day cigarette habit, he had to undergo a heart bypass operation in 1991, but this has done little to affect his enthusiasm for the game.

MODERN EQUIVALENT:
Dennis Bergkamp
HOW MUCH WOULD HE BE WORTH NOW?
£20million

STANLEY MATTHEWS

Popularly known as the 'Wizard of Dribble' because of his silky skills down the right wing, Matthews was born in Stoke in 1915, during the First World War. His playing career began in his hometown in 1932 and spanned four decades, making it one of the longest in football's history.

Despite his extended career Matthews won a relatively small number of honours, although this did not mask the fact he was an incredibly talented individual on the right wing.

His finest hour was the role he played in the Blackpool v Bolton FA Cup Final of 1953. This match has been immortalized as 'The Matthews Final' in honour of his excellent display down the right and deadly supply to the likes of Stan Mortensen (who scored a hat-trick as Matthews' Blackpool won 4-3).

His England career was equally lengthy, starting at the age of 19 in 1934 and finally ending with 54 caps in 1957 at the age of 43! He finally retired in 1965 at the age of 50 having played over 700 league games, winning two Footballer Of The Year awards and a knighthood along the way.

MODERN DAY EQUIVALENT:
Steve McManaman
HOW MUCH WOULD HE BE WORTH NOW? £14million

BOBBY MOORE

Often regarded as the outstanding central defender in the world during the '60s and '70s thanks to his authority at the heart of defence. He also displayed an amazing sense of anticipation and exuded calm and composure, while providing great distribution – often making defence the springboard for attack.

The West Ham centre back joined the club at 17 and became England's youngest captain at 22. But this was only a hint of the glories to come for the Barking born player. Cup success with 'The Hammers', firstly the FA cup in '64, was followed, the next season, by the European Cup Winners' Cup. But the best was yet to come.

All this knockout competition success didn't do Moore any harm when England progressed in the World Cup the following year, winning on home soil against arch rivals Germany.

Moore remained a fixture in the England side until 1973, winning a massive 108 caps. He retired from playing in 1977, but later failed to make an impression as manager. After a battle with cancer, Moore died in 1993, but will live on as one of the true legends of the modern game.

MODERN DAY EQUIVALENT:
Rio Ferdinand – eventually!
HOW MUCH WOULD HE BE WORTH NOW? £12million

MICHEL PLATINI

Generally regarded as one of France's most talented footballers ever. Michel emerged in 1972 from his father's shadow, who was his coach at Nancy. His natural talent shone through and there is no doubt he would have made it regardless of his dad's helping hand.

Despite being a midfielder, he soon established himself as a goalscorer whoever he played for. His tally for Nancy was 98 goals in just 175 appearances.

Michel made the international grade as a 21-year-old, in the first of 72 caps for his country. His amazing strike rate continued, with 41 goals for his country.

His main strengths were vision and the skillful ability to deliver defence splitting passes with uncanny accuracy, along with being a dead ball expert.

As if to prove he could score anywhere, Platini chose to join Juventus in Italy – the toughest league in the world – but still managed to bag a massive 68 goals in 147 appearances.

In his late 20s, Platini reached his peak and was awarded no fewer than three European Footballer Of The Year titles in a row. He played in three consecutive World Cups and very nearly guided France to the Final in 1982 – they fell at the Semi-Final hurdle. However, he made up for that by helping his country to glory at the 1984 European Championships.

He took charge of the French national team in 1987 but failed to live up to expectations as manager.

MODERN DAY EQUIVALENT
David Beckham
HOW MUCH WOULD HE BE WORTH NOW? £18million

JIMMY GREAVES

One of the most prolific and effective goalscorers of all time. Greaves started his career at Chelsea, where he scored on his debut at the age of 17. Two years later he won the first of his 57 England caps. His Chelsea career was a massive success, scoring 124 goals in just 157 games.

Jimmy soon becomes a top target for Italian clubs and was lured away by the lire of AC Milan. He stayed for a mere four months, before opting to join Tottenham, where he rediscovered his scoring touch. Greaves remained an England regular and overcame hepatitis in 1965 to force his way back into Alf Ramsey's England team for the World Cup. Greaves was selected in the early stages of the tournament, but was injured in the Quarter-Final against Argentina.

Greaves then had to experience the crushing disappointment of missing the most important match of his life: the World Cup Final. Hurst hat-trick. The rest is history.

Greaves' last match in an England shirt took place a short time after that incident in 1967. Jimmy ended up with an impressive statistic of 44 goals from 57 international games. He then rapidly slipped out of the game at the top level and in 1971 announced his retirement at the age of 31.

MODERN DAY EQUIVALENT: Alan Shearer
HOW MUCH WOULD HE BE WORTH NOW? £16million

FRANZ BECKENBAUER

Also known as 'The Kaiser'. Franz was a commanding German star who halfway through his distinguished international career convinced his country's manager to play him as an attacking sweeper – it was a move which massively influenced football tactical thinking from then on.

'The Kaiser' made his name at club level with Bayern Munich and two years later received the first of his 103 international caps in 1965. Franz found himself on the losing side in the famous 1966 World Cup Final, but ultimately got his revenge in 1970 by not only knocking out England 3-2 in the Quarter-Finals, but by winning nearly every honour and competition available – twice European Footballer Of The Year, three European Cups, a World Cups and a European Championship.

At the end of his 25-year playing career, Beckenbauer made the natural progression to coach of West Germany. He won the World Cup with them in 1990, eventually beating a lacklustre Argentina side in the Final in Italy. He then decided to return to club football in 1993 with his beloved Bayern Munich.

MODERN DAY EQUIVALENT:
Sol Campbell
HOW MUCH WOULD HE BE WORTH NOW?
£12million

UMBRO
SHARP

ALL THE TOP INFO ON ALL YOUR FAVE STARS!

NO.11

ROY KEANE

MAN UTD

ON BEING A WINNER WITH UNITED

"You get greedier every season. When I look back on my career I want to have as many medals as possible and I'll never tire of winning things. The desire to carry on winning keeps you sharp. Winning trophies becomes a habit and one you don't want to break."

ON THE IMPORTANCE OF SUCCESS IN EUROPE

"Europe is obviously our No.1 target. People say that getting to the Final will be a success, but we don't just want to get to the Final, we want to win it. No-one remembers the losers – you've got to get your hands on that trophy."

ON THE PRESSURE OF BEING AT THE TOP

"Real pressure in football is fighting it out at the bottom of the league, not chasing major trophies. That's a really nice form of pressure and one that we love here at United."

ON CONCENTRAING ON WINNING THE CHAMPIONS LEAGUE

"I think fans worry that we play down the domestic league. I can assure the fans that we always want to win the league."

ON INJURING HIS KNEE LAST SEASON

"When it happened I wondered if I would ever play again. As I lay on the turf I suspected it was something serious because I heard something snap in my knee. Although it was hard to sit and see Man United come away empty handed last season, I'm glad that I can help them this season."

ON BEING THE CAPTAIN OF MAN UNITED

"It's a great honour, but it doesn't change how I perform on the pitch – I still go in for the tackles! I think as Captain I need to calm down a little – some of my sendings off in the past have been silly. It's something I try to work on controlling in my game – the problem is I prefer it when the tackles come flying in!"

ON CLUB & COUNTRY MANAGERS

"Out of the four I've had in my career they have all added something to my game and made me a better player. At Nottingham Forest Brian Clough was brilliant for me. He was a great motivator – he told you off when you deserved it, but praised you when you did well. Alex Ferguson is another you have to have great respect for. He will give you a right rollocking if you have played badly, but he is always right. With the Ireland team both Jack Charlton and Mick McCarthy are top managers."

ON THE REPUBLIC OF IRELAND TEAM

"We just missed out at Euro '96 and France '98 which was bitterly dissapointing, but I think Mick McCarthy has had a lot of rebuilding to do. With the amount of good young players coming through I think we will come good again. Playing in the World Cup in 1994 was a fantastic experience. Hopefully, I can lead them to Belgium 2000 and Japan 2002."

ON THE PLAYERS HE ADMIRED MOST AS A LAD

"As a kid I supported Spurs and in that era I looked to Glenn Hoddle – I was amazed by his skills. But obviously I'm a different kind of player to that, so I ended up looking up to people like Bryan Robson."

ON HAVING TO WATCH SPURS ON TV WHEN HE WAS YOUNG

"Living in Ireland it was impossible to go and watch Tottenham. Everyone supported Liverpool or Man Utd, so I supported Spurs to be different. I still take an interest in what they're doing, but nothing like I used to. It's a shame they've been doing so badly for so long. "

EUROPEAN CUP-WINNERS' CUP 1998
CHELSEA v VFB STUTTGART

MAY 13th, 1998
CHELSEA 1-0 VFB STUTTGART (HT: 0-0)

CHELSEA: De Goey, Petrescu, Clarke, Leboeuf, Duberry, Granville, Poyet (sub: Newton), Wise, Di Matteo, Flo (sub: Zola), Vialli. Scorer: Zola
VFB STUTTGART: Wohlfahrt, Yakin, Berthold, Hagner (sub: Ristic), Haber (sub: Djordjevic), Schneider (sub: Endress), Soldo, Poshner, Akpoborie, Bobic, Balakov.
REFEREE: S. Braschi (Italy)
ATTENDANCE: 30,216 (in Stockholm)

STAR MAN GIANFRANCO ZOLA

Because of injury it was a surprise to many that Gianfranco Zola was fit enough to play any sort of role in Chelsea's first European Final for 27 years. But the Italian international proved his value and his fitness by coming off the bench after 71 minutes and scoring the winner with only his second touch, following a superb through pass from skipper Dennis Wise. It was no more than Gianluca Vialli's men had deserved as the west Londoners were by far the more ambitious of the two sides, shrugging off early pressure to launch a string of attacks on the German side's goal. It was all Chelsea in the second half and the only surprise was that 'The Blues' were unable to capitalise on their superiority earlier. It wasn't all plain sailing for Chelsea, however, Romanian star Dan Petrescu was sent off six minutes from the end. But both sides finished the game reduced to ten men as Stuttgart saw midfielder Poshner red carded just before the final whistle.

MOMENT OF THE MATCH

The inspired decision by Chelsea coach Graham Rix to take off Norway international striker Tore Andre Flo and replace him with Gianfranco Zola after 70 minutes. The tiny Italian had been on the field barely 30 seconds when he popped up to score 'The Blues'' vital winner.

HOW THEY MADE THE FINAL

CHELSEA	VFB STUTTGART
R1 1st leg v Slovan Bratisl'va 2-0	R1 1st leg v IBV 3-1
R1 2nd leg v Slovan Bratisl'va 2-0	R1 2nd leg v IBV 2-1
R2 1st leg v Tromso 2-3	R2 1st leg v Germinal Ekeren 4-0
R2 2nd leg v Tromso 7-1	R2 2nd leg v Germinal Ekeren 2-4
QF 1st leg v Real Betis 2-1	QF 1st leg v Slavia Prague 1-1
QF 2nd leg v Real Betis 3-1	QF 2nd leg v Slavia Prague 2-0
SF 1st leg v Vicenza 0-1	SF 1st leg v Loko'tiv Moscow 2-1
SF 2nd leg v Vicenza 3-1	SF 2nd leg v Loko'tiv Moscow 1-0

EVERYTHING YOU WANTED TO KNOW ABOUT

Blackburn had won the league title twice and FA Cup six times earlier this century, but they then had to endure a barren spell of 67 trophyless years. That was ended when they took the Premiership title in 1995 and re-emerged as one of the country's biggest clubs. However, the Ewood Park outfit have struggled since Alan Shearer left in 1996, but are hoping to regain prominence under manager Roy Hodgson. So if you thought their glory days were all rover, read SHOOT's definitive guide and think again!

FORMED: 1875
GROUND: Ewood Park
NICKNAME: 'Rovers'
RECORD LEAGUE VICTORY: 9-0 v Middlesborough November 6th 1954.
MOST LEAGUE APPEARANCES: Derek Fazackerley – 596 (1970-86)
MOST CAPPED PLAYER: Bob Crompton – 41 caps for England.
PLAYER WITH MOST LEAGUE GOALS: Simon Garner – 168 (1978-92).
TOP SCORER 1997/98 (LEAGUE): Chris Sutton 17

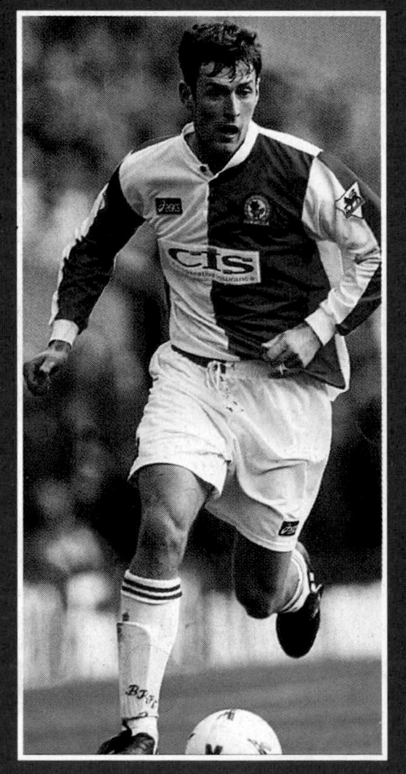

HONOURS: LEAGUE CHAMPIONS: 1911-12; 1913-14; 1994-95. **FA CUP:** 1884; 1885; 1886; 1890; 1891; 1928.

THE COUNTRY'S BIGGEST CLUBS!

GREAT MANAGER KENNY DALGLISH

'King Kenny ' returned to management in 1991. His first season saw Rovers win promotion to the Premiership with a play-off victory against Leicester in 1992. His crowning moment came when Rovers won the title in 1995, back at his old Anfield stomping ground.

WHAT A STAR BLACKBURN'S GREAT PLAYERS

COLIN HENDRY

The Scottish braveheart has witnessed the incredible rise of Rovers from the beginning. He originally moved from Dundee in 1986 and after a brief spell with Manchester City he returned to Ewood Park to win promotion and the Premiership in 1995. Never scared to put his foot in, he has picked up more knocks than your front door and continues to be Blackburn's most competitive player. Starred for Scotland at France '98 last summer.

ALAN SHEARER

'Super Al' was bought for a then record £3.65million by Blackburn from Southampton in 1992. 165 goals and four seasons later, Rovers had won the Premiership and were in the Champions League, largely thanks to his goals. His transfer to Newcastle caused outrage amongst the Ewood faithful, and he has now revealed he was offered a management post to stay at the club. Will Rovers ever see a better goalscorer at the club? It's doubtful.

CHRIS SUTTON

Given the unenviable task of carrying the can for the departed Alan Shearer, Chris Sutton has continued to develop as a player since losing the other half of Blackburn's famous 'SAS' partnership. Although also handy in defence, it is in front of goal that Sutton's true ability is shown. Great in the air, quick on the ground, he's also a born competitor and it shouldn't be forgotten that he was also an integral part of the side that brought the Premiership to Ewood Park.

DID YOU KNOW?

Ewood Park was used to film a Hovis bread television commercial in 1984.

ARE YOU A FOOTIE GENIUS?

THEN PROVE IT BY TACKLING THE SHOOT ANNUAL MEGA QUIZ!

OVER THE NEXT SIX PAGES THERE'S QUESTIONS, PUZZLES AND TEASERS TO STUMP EVEN THE BIGGEST SOCCER KNOW ALL. SEE HOW MANY YOU CAN GET RIGHT THEN CHECK YOUR ANSWERS AT THE END! PENS 'N' PAPER AT THE READY...

Check out the pics below and see if you can work out who they are. To help you there's a clue under each photo. Give yourself two points for every correct answer.

1. THIS WELSH DRAGON IS A REAL WING WIZARD.

2. HE WON THE TITLE BEFORE BECOMING A MAGPIE.

3. SCORED THE GOAL OF THE TOURNAMENT AT FRANCE '98.

4. NOT A VERY POPULAR PERSON IN TUNISIA!

5. HE WENT FROM LOFTUS ROAD TO UPTON PARK.

6. HE'S THE BOSS OF THE BRIDGE.

7. SHOT STOPPER FOR THE WORLD CHAMPS.

8. THE WORLD'S GREATEST PLAYER?

9. BRISTOL, NEWCASTLE, MANCHESTER – HE'S BEEN AROUND A BIT.

10. A WINNER WITH UNITED, A WORLD CUP SINNER WITH ENGLAND.

UP FOR THE CUP

USING YOUR COOL CUP KNOWLEDGE TACKLE THESE TEN TROPHY RELATED TEASERS. AWARD YOURSELF ONE MARK FOR EVERY CORRECT ANSWER.

1. Who won both the FA Cup and the League Cup in 1993?
2. Which team won the FA Cup in 1996?

3. Which nation won the 1990 World Cup in Italy?
4. Who did Chelsea beat when they won the FA Cup in 1997?
5. When did Everton last win the FA Cup?

6. How many times have Newcastle United won the FA Cup?
7. Which team did Liverpool beat in their last League Cup Final win?

8. In what year did Man United win the FA Cup after going to a replay against Crystal Palace?
9. Who did Wimbledon beat in their last FA Cup Final win back in 1988?
10. Who were the last team outside the top division to win the FA Cup?

WHOSE BADGE IS IT ANYWAY?

CAN YOU WORK OUT THE TEAMS TO WHOM THESE TEN BADGES BELONG? THERE'S A POINT FOR EVERY CORRECT ANSWER.

WORDSPOT I

Can you find the names of the following Premiership 'keepers in the grid below. They're hidden vertically, horizontally and diagonally. Give yourself a point for every name you find.

BOSNICH • DE GOEY • FLOWERS • GIVEN • ILIC • JAMES • MARTYN • SEAMAN • SCHMEICHEL • WALKER

B	S	W	J	N	I	M	F	G	S	N	G
O	N	M	A	R	T	Y	N	N	T	E	I
S	M	H	M	Z	A	E	T	V	A	H	V
N	K	T	E	N	K	S	R	T	D	F	E
I	V	G	S	L	D	F	P	I	B	G	N
C	S	C	H	M	E	I	C	H	E	L	D
H	R	J	C	Y	G	H	C	W	C	N	Y
Z	U	E	N	F	O	B	T	Z	A	K	P
P	W	A	L	K	E	R	O	M	H	X	I
T	Q	O	N	R	Y	A	A	N	M	Y	L
F	P	F	L	O	W	E	R	S	T	P	I
G	A	U	I	C	S	C	R	K	J	F	C

ODD ONE OUT

WHO IS THE ODD ONE OUT FROM THE FOLLOWING LISTS OF PLAYERS. YOU GET A POINT FOR IDENTIFYING THE PLAYER AND ANOTHER POINT FOR THE REASON.

1. Steve Bruce, Tony Adams, Sol Campbell, Des Walker
2. Steve Lomas, Colin Hendry, Paul Ince, Steve Watson
3. Graham Taylor, Roy Hodgson, Bryan Robson, Bobby Robson
4. Patrick Kluivert, Roberto Baggio, David Beckham, Zinedine Zidane
5. Nottingham Forest, Swindon Town, Bolton Wanderers, Charlton
6. Michael Owen, Zinedine Zidane, Gabriel Batistuta, Paul Scholes
7. Dennis Bergkamp, Paul Ince, Ronaldo, Benito Carbone
8. George Graham, Alex Ferguson, Kenny Dalglish, Howard Wilkinson
9. Ken Monkou, Andy Townsend, Neil Shipperley,
10. Mark Hughes, Gary Pallister, Paul Gascoigne, Graeme Le Saux

WHO ARE YA?!

CAN YOU WORK OUT THE IDENTITIES OF THE PLAYERS FROM THE CLUES BELOW? THERE'S TWO POINTS FOR EACH CORRECT ANSWER.

1. a. He was born in east London.
b. He started his career at The Valley.
c. He was included in Glenn Hoddle's England World Cup squad.
d. He plays in midfield for 'The Magpies'.
e. His surname could also be someone's christian name.

2. a. This player has never appeared for a club based outside London.
b. He started his professional career with Crystal Palace.
c. He missed out on a France '98 place because of injury.
d. He broke the scoring record of a Premiership club last season
e. He's a Gunner turned Hammer.

3. a. His first taste of glory came with Wimbledon.
b. He has a reputation for being one of football's hard men.
c. He has lifted trophies for his current club two seasons running.
d. He's one of the Premiership's smallest stars.
e. He's the captain of 'The Blues'.

4. a. This star began his career with Cambridge United.
b. His move was ruined when he broke his leg just after joining his new team.
c. His career was rescued by a big-spending Midlands club.
d. He can play at the back or up front.
e. He made his England debut against Chile last February.

5. a. He's a *Geordie* lad who started his career with a north-east club.
b. After impressing there he headed for north London.
c. An unsuccessful spell in Italy followed after that.
d. His wild antics have got him in trouble in the past.
e. He was surprisingly left out of the World Cup for being unfit.

6. a. He came to England from Italy on a free transfer.
b. In his last season with his Italian club he led them to European Cup glory.
c. He spent most of his first season in England on the substitute's bench.
d. He was surprisingly made player/manager of his English club after the departure of their big name boss.
e. He won two trophies in his first season as boss.

7. a. He started his career at Upton Park but left under a cloud.
b. He became the main midfield man at Old Trafford.
c. He then moved to one of Italy's biggest Serie A clubs.
d. He came home and became a red for the second time.
e. He's known as 'The Guv'nor'.

8. a. This Dutch star began his career in Amsterdam.
b. He moved to Italy but didn't really enjoy life there.
c. He then transfered to north London.
d. He was a double winner with his English club last season...
e. ...and was named England's Player Of The Year.

9. a. He began his professional career with Bristol Rovers.
b. But really made his name while he was at Crystal Palace.
c. His impressive form for a Yorkshire club forced him into the England reckoning...
d. ...and it was no surprise when he went to France '98.
e. Unfortunately he didn't get a game.

10. a. He came through the Everton ranks last season.
b. His distinctive dreadlocks made him easy to spot... until he decided to have them all cut off!
c. He scored a wonder goal against his club's biggest rivals, Liverpool.
d. His favourite food is bacon butties and he tucks into them whenever he can.
e. He's a secret Arsenal fan!

WORLD CUP '98

CAST YOUR MIND BACK TO LAST SUMMER AND THE WORLD CUP FINALS IN FRANCE. HOW MUCH OF THE TOURNAMENT CAN YOU REMEMBER? TWO POINTS FOR EACH CORRECT ANSWER.

1. Who scored the first goal of France '98?
2. Who scored the last goal of France '98?
3. How many games did Scotland win during the tournament and how many goals did they score?
4. What do the following countries all have in common? USA, Japan, Tunisia, Scotland.
5. Which two England players missed in the penalty shoot-out with Argentina?
6. What do the following players all have in common? Dunga, Alan Shearer, Didier Deschamps, Paolo Maldini.

7. Which player won the Golden Boot trophy in France, which country does he play for and how many goals did he score?
8. The Final was played between France and Brazil but which countries did they beat in the Semi-Finals?
9. Which French star was sent-off in the second half of the Final for a second bookable offence and what British club does he play for?
10. How many goals did Brazilian superstar Ronaldo score in the tournament and why did he almost miss the Final against France?

WHERE IN THE WORLD?

READ THE TEAM NAMES BELOW AND SEE IF YOU CAN GUESS WHICH COUNTRY THEY COME FROM. GIVE YOURSELF A POINT FOR EVERY CORRECT ANSWER.

1. Silkeborg
2. Lens
3. Wolfsburg
4. Apollon
5. Twente
6. Merida
7. Ebbw Vale)
8. Botafogo
9. San Jose Clash
10. Rotor

WORDSPOT 2

See if you can spot the surnames of ten world class strikers in the grid below. The names can be found horizontally, diagonally or vertically and you get a point for every one you find.

BATISTUTA • BERGKAMP • CASIRAGHI • FLO • IKPEBA • OWEN • RONALDO • SHEARER • SUKER • VIERI

```
Z P S H E A R E R A
C M S P O W C G U T
O A U V I W H K J U
L K S O I K E M N T
F G E I D R P N B S
I R Q D R L L E O I
R E X U R A A K B T
E B P V X Z G N A A
I F W A Y S T H O B
V Y Z R E K U S I R
```

TRANSFER TRAIL

BY READING EACH LIST OF TEAMS DISCOVER THE TRANSFER TRAILS OF A NUMBER OF TOP PLAYERS. HOW MANY CAN YOU IDENTIFY? GIVE YOURSELF TWO POINTS FOR EACH CORRECT ANSWER.

1. QPR – Brentford (loan) – Besiktas (loan) – QPR – Newcastle – Tottenham
2. Watford – Liverpool – Newcastle
3. Tottenham – Middlesbrough – Everton
4. Man United – Barcelona – Bayern Munich (loan) – Man United – Chelsea – Southampton
5. Blackpool – QPR – West Ham
6. Burnley – Chester – Bury – Stoke – Arsenal
7. Crystal Palace – Southend – Nott'm Forest – Liverpool – Aston Villa
8. Wolves – Southampton – Swindon (loan) – Blackburn Rovers
9. Reading – Newcastle – West Ham
10. Torino – Reggiana – Casert – Ascoli – Torino – Napoli – Inter Milan – Sheffield Wednesday